Jan Hus

Reformation in Bohemia

Jan Hus

Reformation in Bohemia

by

Oscar Kuhns and Robert Dickie

REFORMATION PRESS

2017

British Library Cataloguing in Publication Data

ISBN 978-1-872556-29-1

© Reformation Press 2017

Originally published in 1907 as
John Hus: The Witness
This edition edited and annotated
by Dr Robert J Dickie

Published by Reformation Press
11 Churchill Drive, Stornoway
Isle of Lewis, Scotland HS1 2NP

www.reformationpress.co.uk

Printed by www.lulu.com

Also available as a Kindle e-book
ISBN 978-1-872556-28-4

Contents

Foreword

Jan Hus—whose name is sometimes anglicised as John Huss—was born in the south of Bohemia around 1369. His humble beginnings in a small village gave no indication of the important role he would later play as the reformer of the Roman Catholic Church in Bohemia. His continued struggle for reform led to his trial and martyrdom at the stake in 1415.

Hus was ordained as a priest in Prague in 1400 and two years later he began to demand reform of the Church. He was influenced by the writings of John Wycliffe, the 'morning star of the Reformation', who had died in 1384. Hus helped to circulate Wycliffe's books in Bohemia, despite public burning of such literature. Like his English predecessor, Hus denounced the moral degeneracy and corruption of the clergy and bishops, and eventually even the papacy itself. He contended for the laity to receive wine in the Eucharist, and accordingly the Hussites became known as the 'people of the chalice'.

Despite the initial support of his archbishop, Hus came under pressure as the forces of the Roman Catholic Church mustered against him, and the Pope eventually excommunicated him in 1411. Hus went into exile and continued to strive for reform. Whilst staying in a castle during his this period, he translated part of the Bible into Bohemian. The parallels with Luther's life and work are obvious, and indeed, after an initial reluctance to be identified with the Bohemian 'heretics', Luther expressed his debt to Hus and other Bohemians.

This book traces the life and work of Hus and the dawning of reforming work in Bohemia. It also looks at the later history of the Hussites after the martyrdom of Hus and Jerome of Prague at the Council of Constance in 1415.

Why has so little attention been paid to Hus in English popular religious literature? Bohemia and its history are certainly unfamiliar to most English-speaking readers, and this is compounded by difficulties in reading and pronouncing Slavic names. It must also be recognised that the reforming work was incomplete—Hus continued to maintain doctrines and practices which were refuted by later reformers such as Luther, Calvin, Zwingli and Knox. Nevertheless, Hus began the work of reformation and his history and his role in the Bohemian Reformation deserve to be more widely known and appreciated.

Editorial changes in this edition

This book was originally published in 1907 by an American, Prof. Oscar Kuhns. The basic text has been revised to make the style, punctuation and layout contemporary.

Dr Robert Dickie has extensively edited the book and has provided much supplementary material (both within the body of the text and in footnotes) to give useful historical context and relevant topographical information. This has drawn on many written and online resources. In describing locations, the distances from Prague are 'as the crow flies', using approximate directions of the 'eight-point compass'.

A further significant enhancement is an appendix providing thumbnail biographies of people featured in the book. Individuals such as Luther and Calvin simply have their dates of birth and death recorded, as their lives are well known. A short guide to Czech pronunciation has also been included after the author's preface.

In keeping with modern convention, personal names and place names normally appear in the original language, with the exception of commonly anglicised place names such as Bohemia, Constance, Moravia, and Prague. Older anglicised versions of place names and personal names are given in brackets for reference purposes.

The publisher hopes that this book will introduce readers to the fascinating subject of Jan Hus, the Bohemian reformer and a predecessor to the Protestant Reformation.

The Publisher
Stornoway
August 2017

Preface

In writing this book, my aim has been to give a plain, straightforward, and concise account of the life, death, and influence of one of the world's most inspiring witnesses to the truth. In so doing I have used the standard authorities—those which form the basis of every modern discussion of the life of Jan Hus. For the opportunity to use the most indispensable of all these authorities—Hermann von der Hardt's[1] *Rerum Concilii Œcumenici Constantiensis* [*Affairs of the Ecumenical Council of Constance*], František Palacký's[2] *Geschichte von Böhmen* [*History of Bohemia*], and the same author's *Documenta Mag. Johannis Hus* [*Documents of Master Jan Hus*]—I am indebted to the courtesy of the Librarian of Harvard University. In quoting from the proceedings of the Council of Constance—although I have had Von der Hardt constantly on hand for reference—I have used Jacques Lenfant's[3] *History of the Council of Constance*, which is largely a translation of the former.

Oscar Kuhns

1907

---

[1] Hermann von der Hardt (1660–1746) was a German historian and professor of oriental languages.

[2] Prounounced Frantishek Palatskee. Palacký (1798–1876) was a pre-eminent Czech historian and politician.

[3] Jacques Lenfant (1661–1728) was a French Protestant theologian. He wrote extensively, mostly on historical topics.

Czech pronunciation

Czech is a Slavic language, with few words or names recognisable to English speakers. Furthermore, it includes letters which do not feature in Western European languages.

Readers are naturally curious about the pronunciation of unfamiliar names. In this book, an approximate pronunciation is given for the first instance of a name (and this is replicated in the appendix) using common 'English' sounds rather than the academically orientated International Phonetic Alphabet (IPA). To reduce complexity, Czech letters not appearing in this book are omitted from the following pronunciation guide.

The pronunciation of Czech vowels is generally similar to English: a as in bat, e as in bet, i (or y) as in bit or beet, o as in bot and u as in but or boot. Vowels with an acute accent (á, í/ý, ó, ú) are simply prolonged forms of the unaccented vowels. In the final syllable of a word, the letter ú is written as ů.

The consonants g and s are as in 'gate' and 'sing' (not as in 'general' or 'basic'), and the letter r is lightly trilled as in Scottish English.

Most consonants sound similar to their English counterparts. However, at the end of a word and in some other situations, certain consonants are pronounced less forcefully—*e.g.*, d is pronounced as t and v as f. The prepositions z and ze (English: from) fuse with the following word in pronunciation, and they modify the final syllable of the word.

The following consonants are pronounced differently from the English ones: c is ts (as in bats) and j is y (as in you). The double consonant ch is pronounced as in Scottish 'loch' and is transliterated as ch.

Czech contains six letters with a small accent sign (ˇ) above the letter: č is transliterated tsh (as in church), ě is transliterated ye (as in yes), ň is transliterated ny (as in canyon), ř is transliterated rzh (trilled r followed by the zh sound in measure), š is transliterated sh (as in shut), and ž is transliterated zh (as in measure). In alphabetical ordering, Czech treats these letters (and ch) as separate letters, but this has been ignored in the appendix to simplify listings for English-speaking readers.

The Editor

Chapter 1

Forerunners of the Reformation

The materials for a biography of Jan Hus are comparatively meagre. Practically nothing is known of his early years, and the biographer is confined to the narration of the oft-repeated story of his quarrel with the Roman Catholic hierarchy and his trial, condemnation, and execution at Constance,[4] together with a more or less complete analysis of his reforming teachings.

Yet Hus occupies a peculiar position in the history of the development of evangelical religion. In many respects, he may be said to have begun the Reformation, and if circumstances had been favourable, Hussitism and not Lutheranism might have been the great antagonist of Roman Catholicism throughout the succeeding centuries.

This was not to be. A combination of circumstances—historical, social, and religious—prevented Hus becoming the leader of modern Protestantism, just as they had prevented Wycliffe do-

---

[4] The name of the German city is Konstanz. However, as the Council is known to the English-speaking world as the Council of Constance, the name of the city has been given in its English spelling. The city lies in the state of Baden-Württemberg in southwestern Germany. It is located at the western end of Lake Constance (German: Bodensee).

ing so a few years before. The world had to wait a further hundred years before the final break with Rome was to occur. Yet if Hus was not the first of the new dispensation, he was the most influential, as he was the last of the forerunners of the Reformation. He was literally the morning star leading the way to the full daylight of evangelical doctrine, which, through the influence of Luther and others, then spread over the whole world.

It is a natural tendency to look upon all great movements, as suddenly bursting forth, without any previous announcement. However, such movements are rarely the invention of one man or of many men, but rather they are the end result of a step-wise process.

The same thing is true of the Reformation. It was not entirely the work of Luther or Zwingli or Calvin; the times and even the seasons were ripe—Paul had planted, Apollos watered, and God gave the increase.

Protesting against Roman Catholicism

The root idea of Protestantism is a protest against the great hierarchy of Rome, against the substitution of rites and ceremonies for heart religion, and against the abuse of priestly power, especially in the selling of spiritual benefits for money. In Luther these things were summed up, first, in the great doctrine that 'the just shall live by faith', which he opposed to the great mass of works of supererogation; and secondly, in the doctrine of the authority of the Bible, which he opposed to the claim of papal infallibility. However, there was little that was new in these doctrines of Luther. Individually and collectively, these doctrines had been proclaimed repeatedly by holy men throughout the Dark Ages and Middle Ages, until we reach Jan Hus, by whom the authority of the Bible, if not justification by faith, was once for all laid down as an incontrovertible fact. It is, therefore, of value—indeed, it is the only reasonable way to make Hus's work stand out in bold relief—to trace the development of Protestant doctrines up to his time.

Professor Harnack, a church historian, wrote, 'The Christian religion is something simple and sublime. It means one thing and one only—eternal life in the midst of time, by the strength and under the eyes of God. His message is great and powerful, because so simple and yet so rich; so simple as to be exhausted in each of the leading thoughts he uttered, so rich that every one of these thoughts seems inexhaustible and the full meaning of the sayings and parables beyond our reach. He himself stands behind everything he said. His words speak to us across the centuries with the freshness of the present. The kingdom of God comes by coming to the individual, by entering into his soul and laying hold of it. It is the rule of the holy God in the hearts of individuals. It is God himself, in his power. This is seen in all Jesus' parables. It is not a question of angels or devils, thrones and principalities, but of God and the soul, the soul and its God.'

Such is the essence of the Christian religion. It needs no words of mine to point out the vast difference between this view of the Church of Christ and that held for so many centuries and even today by the Roman Catholic Church.

The corruption of Christianity

The teaching of Jesus, simple as it is and perfect in its purity, was yet proclaimed in a hostile world incapable of taking it at once and assimilating it to itself. Like all other things, it had to grow and develop. It had to overcome obstacles, many and powerful, before it could become universally accepted and be put into practice. In the course of the struggle, men changed the teaching of Jesus, and for a time Christianity lost its primitive purity. There is no more striking phenomenon in the history of civilisation than the gradual transformation of the simple gospel of Christ into the world-overshadowing hierarchical system of the Church of Rome during the Middle Ages. Christ taught that God was a spirit, and yet, by a certain kind of return to paganism, we see this divine spirit localised and materialised in the images of the saints and in the deification of the priest, and especially of the pope. Again, we see the freedom of the spirit, the grace and love and mercy of God the Father, give way to Pelagianism, 'the theory of salvation by works, adhesion to doctrinal formula, sacramental usage, priestly absolution, outward mortification, and monkish asceticism'.

In consequence of these influences, a great change came over the Church at a very early stage. An ecclesiastical community was formed, clergy and laymen were separated, and the doctrine was firmly established that men could approach God only through priestly mediation. Faith was changed to belief in the Church, and love for Christ was replaced by loyalty to the Church. It was claimed and universally accepted that God had deputed his powers and prerogatives to the pope and the hierarchy, and little by little the gospel became no longer one of hope and love, but of fear. It is no use to utter diatribes against this state of things. It was the necessary historical result of the confusion produced by the coming together of elements so powerful and so diverse as paganism, Judaism, and Christianity. To these we may add the element of barbarism injected into the seething mass during the Migration Period (also known as the Barbarian invasions) in the middle of the first millennium AD.

It was only by compromise that the Roman Catholic Church could maintain the unequal fight—only by substituting saint-worship for idolatry, by retaining the spectacular charm of incense and candles, and by adapting to itself the tremendous prestige of the Roman Empire.

The Church Fathers

Despite this, all along there were men and religious bodies who regarded the emergence of the Roman Catholic Church with distrust and disfavour—they looked back with longing toward the primitive simplicity of the apostolic times, and sought to bring the Church of Rome away from its idolatry and back to the simple doctrines of Christ. The essence of Protestantism is the clearing away the barnacles of superstition, formalism, and lust of power in order to reveal the truth as it is in Christ Jesus. Moreover, this effort had been going on for centuries before the Reformation, in the bosom of the Roman Catholic Church itself—generally, although not always, under the stigma of 'heresy'.

All along there had been men whose lives were filled with spiritual power, such as Clement of Alexandria, Tertullian, and especially Augustine. No more beautiful scene exists in religious literature than that described by Augustine in his *Confessions*, when he and his mother, a few days before her death, leaning on the window of their lodgings at Ostia, discoursed together with a marvellous sweetness of spiritual things, their hearts strangely warmed within them as they talked of God and the soul.

Undoubtedly, then, all through the Dark and Middle Ages there were individuals still filled with the simple religion of the apostolic days.

The Albigensians

It is not, however, until we reach the twelfth century that we find regular, organised and widely spread sects within the bosom of the Roman Catholic Church. The hierarchy of the Church viewed these sects as dangerous.

The most notorious of these were the Cathars. From the town of Albi, in south-western France, where they were especially numerous, they received the name of Albigensians. In addition to holding the old heretical Manichaean doctrine of the good and the evil principle in the universe (a doctrine which often led them to the most fanatical eccentric views), they demanded that the Church should return to the simplicity of the apostolic times. Furthermore, they opposed the supreme authority of the pope, opposed infant baptism, and wished to abolish rich churches, mass and the priesthood. They were ascetics, who refused to take oaths and repudiated auricular confession.

The Albigensians lasted from the eleventh to the fourteenth century, and they were numerous in southern France, northern Italy, and Germany. They reached their high water mark about the year 1200. History provides no more terrible example of the *odium theologicum*[5] than the Albigensian crusade, which was started by Dominic de Guzmán (the founder of the Dominican monastic order) and carried out to its bitter end by Simon de Mont-

---

[5] A Latin phrase which means 'theological hatred'. It refers to the frequently intense anger and hatred generated by disputes over theology.

22

fort, the 5th Earl of Leicester. At Carcassonne in southern France, four hundred were burnt alive. The papal legate and inquisitor, Arnaud Amalric, led the crusade against the Albigensians in southern France. At the siege of Béziers, when a crusader asked how they should distinguish the 'faithful' from the 'heretics', he cried, 'Kill, kill! The Lord will know his own.' According to Arnaud's own shameless account, 'Our men spared no one, irrespective of rank, sex or age, and put to the sword almost 20,000 people. After this great slaughter the whole city was despoiled and burnt.'

The Waldensians

Still more famous and far more influential on later reformers were the Waldensians. Some say that they were the same as the Cathars. However this may be, the movement seems to have been started in 1160 by Peter Waldo of Lyons (hence his followers were called Waldensians or the Poor Men of Lyons). They differed from the Cathars in rejecting the Manichaean doctrine of good and evil spirits.

The Waldensians refused to take oaths, repudiated capital punishment, claimed the right of the laity to consecrate the host (thus rendering unnecessary a regularly ordained priesthood), and they boldly proclaimed their belief that the Roman Catholic Church was not the Church of Christ. They agreed with the Cathars in using the New Testament alone as the basis of their conduct. Furthermore, they condemned the possession of all property, denied the temporal power of the pope, and declared that the existing Church was not necessary to the worship of God.

It has been claimed that the Waldensians originated in apostolic times. This is not true, yet the slow preparation for their doctrines was the work of ages, and many of the prominent tenets can be found in the preceding centuries.

The Waldensians were subjected to fierce persecutions, were driven out of France, and fled to the mountains of northern Italy, where their descendants still exist. Some of them even went so far as Germany and Bohemia.[6] In this latter country they undoubtedly exerted some influence in preparing the way for the great Hussite movement in the fifteenth century. After the Reformation in the sixteenth century, the Waldensians became part of the Reformed branch of Protestantism.

Movements in Italy

Among the most revolutionary of mediaeval 'heretics' was Arnaldo di Brescia [Arnold of Brescia], who died in 1155. He boldly opposed the claims to universal supremacy on the part of the pope. He declared that the Roman Catholic Church must return to the purity and simplicity of apostolic times in order that the world should live in peace.

All these 'reformers' were stigmatised as 'heretics'. Their doctrines were anathematised by the Church, and they themselves were excommunicated and persecuted with all the cruelty that the human mind could invent. Yet within the bosom of the Roman Catholic Church itself, there arose from time to time men who had in many respects the same doctrines, and yet who

---

[6] In a historical context, the lands of the Bohemian Crown as established by Emperor Karel IV in the 14th century. This includes territories like Upper and Lower Lusatia and the whole of Silesia. It is larger than the present-day region of Bohemia in the Czech Republic.

remained loyal and obedient to the established order of the Church.

One of the strangest of these men was Gioacchino da Fiore.[7] According to him there were three periods to the history of the world—the first period, that of the Father, was represented by the Old Testament; the second, that of the Son, was represented by the New Testament; the third, that of the Holy Ghost, was to begin in 1260, when mankind should become purified, all self-ishness should disappear, and men should no longer struggle for the possession of worldly goods. The influence of Gioacchino in the following centuries was enormous, and was largely responsi-ble for the many prophecies and visions that mark the thirteenth and fourteenth centuries. His true followers, however, were among the branch of the Franciscan order known as the Spiritu-als.

In view of the widespread interest in Francis of Assisi, it seems hardly necessary to say much of him here. Yet in many points of his own life, and especially in the development of certain branches of the Franciscan order founded by him, Francis had no small influence in preparing the way for a religion of the heart as opposed to one of mere form. After his death his mo-nastic order was split up into three factions—the Conventuals, composed of those who demanded a liberal interpretation of his rule; the Fraticelli, who demanded a rigid interpretation of the same; and finally the Spirituals, the most radical of all, who adopted the prophecies of Gioacchino da Fiore, and expected

---

[7] Gioacchino da Fiore (c. 1135–1202) is also known in English as Joa-chim of Fiori or Joachim of Flora.

the final triumph of poverty and the total renovation of the world under the influence of the Holy Ghost.

German mystics

While in general the various monastic orders became more and more corrupt, yet in the fourteenth century, and especially in Germany, there were many groups of persons within the Franciscan, Dominican, and Augustinian orders, whose conduct and aspirations were not unlike those of the Pietists in the seventeenth century. Through them, a revival of spiritual religion swept through Germany, and their influence was closely connected with the beginnings of Luther's Reformation.

Chief among them was Eckhart von Hochheim, commonly called Meister [Master] Eckhart, who flourished about the year 1325.[8] He had close relations with the lay religious order of the Beghards and the Brethren of the Free Spirit.[9] He was a man of great speculative talent, and laid down the lines of German mysticism, which were followed by all succeeding mystics. He preached in German on the actual work of the Spirit in the heart. Yet he was not like so many mystics who sought only their own pleasure in the ecstasy of contemplation and the *unio mystica*, the mystical union with God. Eckhart saw the danger of allowing contemplation to degenerate into selfishness. It should

---

[8] Men who graduated as Master of Arts were entitled to use the title 'Master'.

[9] The Beghards were members of a lay religious order. Their members lived in semi-monastic communities but did not take formal religious vows. The Brethren of the Free Spirit were similar, but were noted for Antinomian principles—for this reason Pope Clement V declared them heretical at the Council of Vienne (1311–1312). Both groups flourished in the 13th to 16th centuries.

be not an end in itself, but a source of comfort and strength to meet the battles of life.

Among Eckhart's immediate followers were Jan van Ruusbroec [John van Ruysbroeck] in Flanders and Heinrich Seuse [Henry Suso] in Germany. The latter is one of the most interesting figures in pre-Reformation Church history. He was born in 1295 at Überlingen on Lake Constance, not far from Constance, where Jan Hus suffered martyrdom a little over one hundred years later. Heinrich defended the legacy of Eckhart after Eckhart was posthumously condemned for heresy in 1329.

With Johannes Tauler, we enter into close contact with the Protestant Reformation. His influence on Luther is well known. He was born in Strasbourg about 1300, was a Dominican friar, and was in constant communication with the Friends of God in Basel. He was especially famous as a preacher, and everywhere multitudes came to listen to him. His sermons were full of deep spiritual power, and came from a heart full of love for God and man. The real kernel of his teaching was the indwelling of God in the soul, and his wonderful success was due to his own deep religious experience. As he himself said, 'No man can teach what he has not lived through himself.' His influence on Martin Luther is well known. In Luther's early days of discontent with his religious experience, Johann von Staupitz, the Director-General of the Augustinians advised him to read Tauler's sermons, and he found much comfort in them.

The greatest influence exerted on Luther, however, was by a little book which fell into his hands, which he wrongly thought to be the work of Tauler. Luther published an edition under the title of *Theologia Deutsch*. It was a treatise on heart religion, which showed how sin in its essence is selfishness. Its object was to give a practical turn to the teachings of Eckhart, but it should be noted that Calvin rejected the work as erroneous.

All the German mystics of the fourteenth century remained in the bosom of the Church, however, and confined themselves to the exemplification and promulgation of a pure emotional religion, combined with an ascetic manner of living. They carefully refrained from criticising the Church itself, either in its doctrines or its outer form and observances.

John Wycliffe

Although all the above-mentioned forerunners of the Reformation had so many ideas in common with those of Hus and Luther, yet the connection is only occasional, and by no means organic. With Wycliffe, however, we begin the definite chain of events which, passing through Hus, found a culmination in Luther, Zwingli and Calvin.

John Wycliffe was born in Yorkshire, England, in 1320. He was educated at Oxford, and became one of the most able philosophers of his day. It was through his philosophy that he first became known in Bohemia, and strange as it may seem to us today, the fact that Hus was a follower of the philosophy of Wycliffe had a powerful influence in bringing about his destruction.

The condition of the Roman Catholic Church filled Wycliffe with disgust and indignation. The year 1378 was the turning point in his career, owing to the schism brought about by the election, in September of that year, of Clement VII in opposition to Urban VI.[10] Wycliffe attacked the whole principle of the papacy, as the root of all evils which then burdened Christendom. He translated the Bible into English prose and sent forth a number of poor priests to teach the gospel to the people, all of which produced a profound commotion throughout England. On the one hand, the common people heard them gladly, whereas on the other hand, the rich and influential clergy were filled with rage and hate.

Among the epoch-making teachings of Wycliffe which later were taken up more or less completely by the various divisions of Protestantism were the following: sin deprives a man from possessing anything; all property should be held in common; spiritual power should be entirely separate from the civil; the Church should hold no property; excommunication was of no effect, except the subject of it were in sin, and in no case should it be promulgated for any offence connected with temporal affairs. Wycliffe denied transubstantiation, but held the same erroneous doctrine as Luther did later—consubstantiation. As we shall see later, some of these doctrines Hus accepted, others he did not.

Wycliffe escaped martyrdom in his lifetime. His doctrine concerning the Lord's Supper was published in 1381. It was condemned by the University of Oxford, and a Church Council was

---

[10] The election of Clement VII began the Western Schism. After his death in 1394, the second and final Avignon antipope was elected, Benedict XIII. Four years later, France withdrew recognition of the Avignon papacy but Benedict continued to consider himself as pope. The Council of Constance was designed to bring the Schism to an end, but Benedict refused to stand down in 1415. The Council excommunicated him in 1417 but he refused to recognise this and fled to his native Aragon, where continued to consider himself pope until his death.

called in order to put him on trial. Though he was cited to appear at Rome, he never went there. He was struck with paralysis on 28th December 1384, and died on New Year's eve. In 1415 the Council of Constance condemned his works, and thirteen years later, in 1428, his body was dug up and burned.[11] His influence did not last long in England, but through Hus his doctrines became known to Luther, and played an important part in the great movement of the Reformation on the Continent.

---

[11] The Council of Constance was the Sixteenth Ecumenical Council of the Roman Catholic Church, and lasted from 1414 to 1418. The Council ended the Western Schism, by deposing or accepting the resignation of the papal claimants and electing Pope Martin V. In addition to condemning the works of Wycliffe, the Council tried and condemned Hus and Jerome of Prague. They were both martyred immediately after their trials.

Chapter 2

Political, social and religious conditions of Bohemia

The reformation inaugurated by Jan Hus and the events which followed cannot be clearly understood without some general idea of the state of politics, society, and religion in Bohemia towards the end of the fourteenth century. Similarly, we cannot understand these conditions themselves without having some idea of their gradual development.

It is only by reference to the national history of Bohemia that we can get a clear conception of the complex problems involved in the whole movement of Hussitism. We must know once for all that this movement was not the work of one man, however powerful his influence was, but it was intimately connected with national and religious traditions. The patriotism of a people threatened with being swamped by foreign immigration, joined to the tenacity with which all men cling to the customs of their fathers, made Bohemia a fertile soil for the doctrines of the Waldensians and Wycliffe to take root and grow up. Contemporary events, imperial and papal schisms, and the general corruption of the Roman Catholic Church, all reached a climax just at the time when a man was sent by God to teach the truth and to become the leader of countless thousands.

The political history of Bohemia

The Bohemians are of Slavic origin. The land itself was first inhabited by a Celtic tribe, the Boii, then by a Germanic tribal confederation, the Marcomanni, who were then driven out by the Huns and settled in the land now known as Bavaria. The Slavs, who were allies of the Huns, settled in the land left vacant by the Marcomanni.

For long centuries, the country was ruled by native kings, but in 1310 the male line died out. The sister of the last Slav king, Václav[12] III [Wenceslaus III], had married a son of Heinrich VII [Henry VII] of Luxembourg,[13] and so a German dynasty was seated on the throne of Bohemia. The new king ruled as Jan Lucemburský[14] [John of Luxembourg] from 1310 until 1346.[15] In this way, Bohemia became intimately connected with the various providential circumstances affecting Germany. Karel IV [Charles IV] succeeded Jan Lucemburský as king of Bohemia in 1347. When Karel was subsequently elected as Holy Roman

---

[12] Pronounced Vatslaf.

[13] The House of Luxembourg was late medieval European royal family, whose members between 1308 and 1437 ruled as Kings of the Romans and Holy Roman Emperors as well as Kings of Bohemia and Hungary.

[14] Pronounced Yan Lootsemboorskee.

[15] He was later known as John the Blind, having progressively lost his sight around the age of forty. He died fighting the English at the Battle of Crécy in 1346.

Emperor[16] in 1355, Bohemia was then drawn into the complex relations of imperial politics.

The social history of Bohemia

The history of Bohemia during all this time had been one of almost unceasing progress in prosperity. The native kings, such as Otakar I [Ottokar I] (1155–1230, who reigned discontinuously between 1198 and 1230) and Otakar II [Ottokar II] (c. 1233–1278, reigned 1253–1278), had raised the country to a position of influence throughout the whole of Western Europe. But it was especially through Karel IV that Bohemia reached its climax of prosperity. According to the Czech historian, František Palacký, Karel was 'the most popular king who ever ruled in Bohemia. To this day, every Bohemian heart warms at the mention of his name, and all lips overflow with reverence and gratitude toward the memory of a ruler who, in the tradition of the people, has become the representative of the highest glory and prosperity of his fatherland.'

The emperor seemed to have a special love for the land of his mother,[17] and he devoted his best interests toward building it

---

[16] The term 'Holy Roman Empire' was first used in the 13th century. It consisted of a group of countries in central Europe. The borders of the 'empire' varied throughout the centuries and it was dissolved in 1806 when the last emperor abdicated following a military defeat by Napoleon at the Battle of Austerlitz. Appointment to the office of Holy Roman Emperor was traditionally by election, although it was frequently controlled by dynasties. The German prince-electors, the highest-ranking noblemen of the empire, usually elected one of their peers as 'King of the Romans', and he would later be crowned emperor by the pope. The tradition of papal coronations was discontinued in the 16th century.

up. He made it strong financially, improved agriculture, commerce, and industry, favoured the arts and sciences, and regulated justice, morals and religion. Karel made Prague the beautiful city it is today. He laid the foundations of the famous Charles Bridge [Karlův most[18]], and built many churches and castles. Æneas Sylvius Bartholomeus, who afterward became Pope Pius II, declared that he had seen no land which could compare with Bohemia in the number and magnificence of its buildings.

The most important event of Karel's activity in this respect, and one of the deepest importance for the work of Hus, was the founding of the University of Prague on 7th April 1348.[19] This was the first of the German universities, and became almost immediately an attraction to students from all parts of northern Europe, including France and England. In 1408 the number of students is said to have amounted to thirty thousand. It was organised after the model of the University of Paris, and consisted of four faculties—Theology, Law, Medicine and Philosophy. The university was divided into four parts, called 'nations', depending on the national origin of the students—the Bohemian (including Moravia and Hungary), Bavarian (including Austria, Swabia, Franconia, and the Rhineland), Polish (including Sile-

---

[17] Karel's father, Jan Lucemburský, was from the German dynasty of the House of Luxembourg. His mother was Eliška Přemyslovna (pronounced Elishka Przhemyslovna) [Elizabeth of Bohemia] (1292–1330), the first wife of Jan Lucemburský.

[18] Pronounced Karloof Mosst.

[19] Pope Clement IV issued a Bull in 1347, establishing the university, which was the first in Central Europe. Karel IV accorded the university certain privileges and immunities in 1348, and Prague University (also known as Charles University) opened in 1349. Most Czech sources prefer to give 1348 as the year when the university was founded, rather than 1347 or 1349.

sia,[20] Lithuania, and Russia), and Saxon (including Thuringia, Upper and Lower Saxony, Denmark and Sweden). It will be noticed in the above arrangement that the Bohemians were far outnumbered by foreigners of various sorts, and especially by the Germans. This was to have an important effect on the reforming movement started by Hus a few years later.

Influences on Hus

The question as to where Jan Hus got his reforming ideas has been widely discussed. Some have declared that the Waldensians, who had been driven out of France and who were scattered over all Northern Europe—including Bohemia—sowed the seed of the evangelical movement, which Hus made his own. There is but little basis of truth in this theory, although doubtless Waldensian doctrines did affect Hussitism, especially the different sects into which it was split up after the death of Hus. A much stronger case has been made out by those who claim that Hus only transplanted the doctrines of Wycliffe from England to Bohemia. Yet this bald statement, leaving out of consideration all indigenous events, goes too far. There is no doubt about the vast influence of Wycliffe on Bohemian thinkers. Hus's works are more or less justly said to be a compilation of extracts from those of Wycliffe, and it is doubtful whether Hus would have been burned at the stake, had it not been for the condemnation of Wycliffe's doctrines by the Council of Constance.

---

[20] A historical region of Central Europe, located mostly in present-day Poland, with small parts in the Czech Republic and Germany. Czech Silesia is one of the historical 'Czech lands', together with Bohemia and Moravia.

The relations between Bohemia and England were close. Anna Lucemburská[21] [Anne of Bohemia], sister of King Václav IV [Wenceslas IV], had married Richard II of England in 1382. She had favoured Wycliffe and encouraged him in the translation of the Bible into English. Many students went from Bohemia to Oxford and brought back the doctrines of the English reformer. This was true especially of Jerome of Prague, destined later to be a fellow martyr with Hus. Jerome graduated from the University of Prague in 1398 and later studied at Oxford University, where he became familiar with Wycliffe's teachings.

Hus himself became an earnest student of Wycliffe's works, especially of his philosophical doctrines. The chief accusation against him at Constance, expressed or implied, was that he was a follower of the English 'heretic'. Yet Wycliffe alone could not have produced the Hussite movement, if it had not been for other causes, which chiefly pertained to the national conditions in Bohemia. Many points of difference in doctrine exist between Wycliffe and Hus, who only approved of certain of the Englishman's teachings, and especially differed from him about the doctrine of transubstantiation. Wycliffe, then, was only one— although a very important one—of the elements which make up the Reformation of Hus.

The religious history of Bohemia

In order to understand the violent passions aroused by this movement, we must now cast a glance at the religions and racial conditions of Bohemia. Otakar II had brought large numbers of German colonists to Bohemia in the second half of the thirteenth century, and thus laid the foundation of the inevitable

---

[21] Pronounced Anna Lootsemboorska.

struggle between Slavs and Teutons, which became later so fierce and bitter. German numbers increased greatly after the accession of Karel IV to the throne in 1347, and especially after the founding of the University of Prague in 1348. The majority of the vast number of students who flocked to Prague were Germans, and they naturally made use of their numerical superiority to monopolise the power in all university matters.

Not only in scholastic affairs did the Germans dispute the lead with the Bohemians, however, but also in commerce, business, and even municipal government. Prague was crowded with German merchants and bankers, who threatened to swamp the less strenuous Slavic element. From these factors arose bitter strife, engendered by jealousy, patriotism, and race hatred.

Closely connected with these racial differences were the problems raised by religious and ecclesiastical conditions. The Bohemians had been converted to Christianity much later than the other nations of Europe, and when they were thus converted, it was not by such wholesale and violent means as we observe in the case of the Franks and Saxons. The chief influence on Bohemia had come from Constantinople, and of especial importance were the labours of the two brothers, Cyril and Methodius, from Thessalonica, the great apostles of the Slavic countries.

The union of the Bohemian and Roman Churches

The Slavic origin of the Bohemian Church gave a decided complexion to its customs, traditions, and doctrines, and thus formed an important, though vague, element of the Hussite movement. In the first place, no foreign tongue had been imposed upon them in the church services, in the way that Latin had been in the Roman Catholic Church. A much greater freedom and independence was allowed, as for instance the fact that the priests were at liberty to marry. In outward forms, little effort was made to burden the people with useless ceremonies and extortionate tithes. Such was the condition of things in the early times. However, this condition was to undergo a slow but steady change as soon as the Bohemian Church was united to that of Rome. When the Magyars (Hungarians) attacked Bohemia in the tenth century, both it and Moravia were forced to seek the protection of the German emperor. In this way, a close relationship was established between the two countries, and one result was the merging of the Bohemian Church into that of Rome. From the eleventh century on, the numerous German colonists who flowed into Bohemia brought with them their customs, laws, and government. This naturally resulted in the German form of service—*i.e.*, that of the Roman Catholic Church—gradually superseding that of the Slavs.

Yet the people themselves only slowly yielded to this gradual displacement, especially as it meant giving up their freedom and independence, the substitution of Latin for their native tongue in service and sermons, taking away the individual cup from the people in the Eucharist, and the burden of insatiable calls for ecclesiastical taxes from Rome. As many of the higher clergy were Germans, we can easily see how these two elements, religious and national, tended to keep the common people in a state of protest against the Church, a state that later was changed to fanaticism by the course of events.

Bohemian forerunners of Hus

We have already discussed the religious and national traditions which formed the background to the movement begun by Hus.

We must now turn our attention for a brief time to three men who are known as the forerunners of Hus in Bohemia itself. They laid the foundations on which he built, by proclaiming certain doctrines of a reforming tendency, by laying bare the corrupt condition of the Church and by preparing the vast majority of the Bohemian people to follow the lead of Hus when he should appear.

Konrád Waldhauser

The first of these forerunners of Hus was Konrád Waldhauser [Conrad of Waldhausen], so called from his birthplace, Waldhausen im Strudengau, a small market town in Upper Austria. It was through Karel IV, who was impressed by his learning and energy, that he came to Prague, where he spent many years as preacher at the Church of St Gallus [Czech: kostel sv. Havla] and later at Týn Church [Czech: Týnský chrám]. Konrád enjoyed enormous success. Not only was his church crowded, so that he had to preach in the open square before it, but his sermons, in which he scourged the pride, licentiousness, and avarice of the people, wrought a most remarkable change in the life and conduct of the multitude. Women laid aside their rich garments and costly jewels, men whose conduct had been stained by vice and sin for years repented and lived pious and religious lives. Even greedy moneylenders and public thieves gave up their ill-gotten gains. It was chiefly against the corruption of the clergy that Konrád preached, especially the monks, who at that time were despised and hated throughout the whole Christian world for their overbearing pride, luxury and neglect of duty.

In Konrád's sermons and writings we see already the germs of the essential doctrine of Protestantism—that the gospel should be preached to the people and that outward forms do not ensure salvation. It was no wonder, then, that the clergy cordially hated Konrád. Equally, it was not surprising that the usual weapons in such cases, accusations of heresy, were directed against him. Yet owing to the continued favour shown him by Karel IV he escaped all snares that his enemies laid for him, and he was finally put in charge of the most important parish in Prague, that of the Týn Church, where he died on 8th December 1369.

Jan Milíč z Kroměříže

Still more influential in preparing the way for the Hussite movement was Jan Milíč z Kroměříže[22] [Jan Milíč of Kroměříž], to whom the German church historian August Neander gives the credit of the first impulse toward the Reformation in Moravia.

For many years, Milíč was employed in the Court of Karel IV, and in 1360 was made one of the imperial secretaries. He had everything a man could wish for: he was well off in possessions, and had a good position and the favour of the king. Yet suddenly, in 1363, he declared his intention to renounce all his honours and worldly prosperity in order to serve Christ in poverty and humility. He did this in spite of the earnest remonstrance of his archbishop, Arnošt z Pardubic[23] [Ernest of Pardubice], who said to him, 'What better thing could you do than to help your poor over-shepherd in the care of his flock?' However, Milíč came back to Prague and began to preach in the Old Town of Prague, first in the Church of St Gallus [Czech: kostel sv. Havla], then

---

[22] Pronounced Yan Meeleetsh Zkromyerzheezheh.
[23] Pronounced Arnosht Spardoobeets.

occasionally at St Nicholas [kostel sv. Mikuláše[24]], and finally, from 1364 onwards, at Týn Church. He was the successor of Konrád Waldhauser at St Gallus and the Týn Church.

At first Milíč was not successful, but little by little the interest in his sermons grew until the number of hearers was so great that he had to preach at different places, often three times, or even five times a day. However, not only did he stir the masses with religious enthusiasm, but likewise he won the admiration of the educated classes by his learning and literary talent. He thus became the spiritual director of nearly all Prague. Many of the worst classes of people turned away from a life of sin, and Milíč founded a refuge for penitent women, called New Jerusalem, the expenses of which he paid himself out of funds contributed by charitable persons.

Studying and brooding over the Bible, especially the prophetic books and the Book of Revelation, Milíč believed he had made an important discovery, namely that the prophecy concerning the coming of Christ was to fall within the period 1365–67, and he wrote a learned book about this. He found signs of the Antichrist in all classes and conditions of men, but above all in the clergy, from the archbishop to the lowest monk. This naturally led to hostility from the clergy. Nevertheless, the emperor still kept his kindly feeling toward him. When Milíč appealed against his accusers to Pope Urban V, and went to the papal court himself in 1367, he brought with him a letter of recommendation from the emperor, Karel IV. In spite of this support, Milíč was

---

[24] Pronounced Mikulasheh. This church was the parish church for the Old Town until Týn Church was built.

imprisoned in the monastery of Ara Cœli[25] in Rome, but was released later, and returned to Prague, where he remained for some time. Then in 1374, when the clergy once again accused him of heresy, Milíč went to Avignon, where he fell sick and died before the question of his orthodoxy was settled.

Milíč exerted a mighty influence on the whole Bohemian reform movement. His extraordinary power as a popular preacher stirred the masses of the people to their depths, and prepared the way for the fanaticism of the Hussite Wars[26] after the death of Hus himself. Like Konrád Waldhauser, however, his chief influence was exercised by preaching.

Matěj z Janova

A third man in the list of Hus's forerunners possessed what had been lacking in the other two—that is, the literary skill to spread his doctrines widely throughout the land, far beyond the limits of his own personal influence. This was done by Matěj z Janova[27] [Matthew of Janow] who, unlike his predecessors, was of noble birth, being the son of a Bohemian knight. While he was a student at the University of Prague, he became an earnest follower of Milíč. He had an excellent preparation. After completing his studies at Prague, he spent six years at the University of Paris, where he received the degree of Master of Arts. From

---

[25] The monastery of the Basilica of St Mary of the Altar of Heaven (Latin: Basilica Sanctæ Mariæ de Ara Cœli). During the Middle Ages, this church became the centre of the religious and civil life of Rome.

[26] The wars were fought from 1419 to 1434, initially between the Hussites and European monarchs who sought to enforce the authority of the Roman Catholic Church on them (1420, 1421–22, 1422–23, 1426–27 and 1431). Confrontations between various Hussite factions also occurred towards the end of the period.

[27] Pronounced Mattyey Zyanova.

Pope Urban VI, whom he visited in Rome, he received the position of Canon of the Cathedral Church of Prague.[28] He died on 30th November 1394.

Matěj z Janova was not a pastor or a preacher like Konrád or Milíč, but he exerted his influence chiefly through his writings. By these means he laid the intellectual foundations for Hus's work. Chief among these writings was the *De Regulis Veteris et Novi Testamentis* [*The Principles of the Old and New Testament*]. As Palacký says, considering the real subject of the book, a more appropriate title might have been 'Studies on True and False Christianity'. Although this book is forgotten today, it exerted the most extraordinary influence when it appeared. In it, Matěj discussed the doctrine of the Lord's Supper and advocated the frequent, even daily, administration of the sacrament, and especially the restoration of the custom of the early Church to give to the laity both the wine and the bread. He was in this respect the forerunner of Jakoubek ze Stříbra[29] [Jacob of Stříbro] and

---

[28] Commonly known as St Vitus Cathedral—Katedrála svatého Víta in Czech—a Roman Catholic cathedral in the grounds of Prague Castle. It is the largest church building in the country, and contains the tombs of many Bohemian kings and Holy Roman emperors. Since 1997 it has been known as The Metropolitan Cathedral of Saints Vitus, Wenceslaus and Adalbert (Czech: Metropolitní katedrála svatého Víta, Václava a Vojtěcha).

[29] Jakoubek ze Stříbra (pronounced Yakowbek Zestrzheebra) (1372–1429) was also known as Jacob of Stříbro or Jacob of Mies (the German name for Stříbro). From his small stature he was also called by the Latin name Jacobellus, which means little Jacob. Stříbro (pronounced Strzheebro) is a town in western Bohemia, 67 miles (109 km) southwest of Prague.

the whole Calixtine[30] party, which played so great a part in the later Hussite movement.

In *De Sacerdotum et Monachorum Carnalium Abominatione* [*Concerning the Priesthood and the Abomination of the Flesh of the Monks*] Matěj z Janova scourged the corruption of the times, and in the treatise *De Revelatione Christi et Antichristi* [*Concerning the Revelation of Christ and Antichrist*] he gave the signs of the coming of Antichrist. He declared that Antichrist is not flesh and blood, but spirit—the spirit in the Church that is opposed to the Spirit of Christ. Whosoever works against virtue in unrighteousness or against wisdom and love, and does this knowingly and purposely, he is the Antichrist. The higher position such a man has in the Church, the higher is Antichrist, and if he is head of the Church then he is the highest Antichrist of all. Formerly Antichrist used physical power against the Church, and then he sought to undermine it by heresies; now he shows himself under the form of piety, bedecked with art, science, religion, pomp and circumstance.

Among the signs which Matěj of Janov gave as announcing the coming of Antichrist were the mingling of the spiritual things with the worldly, and the temporal with the eternal, the neglect of duty and general corruption of the clergy, the divisions and schisms in the Church at large (and the bitter contest between Dominicans and Franciscans, priests and monks), together with the prevalence of luxury, dead ceremonies, the worship of imag-

---

[30] The Calixtines were a moderate faction of the Hussites. The name was derived from *calix*, Latin for their emblem, the chalice. They were also known as the Utraquists or Prague Party. Utraquism (from Latin *sub utraque specie*, meaning 'in both kinds') was the principal dogma, and one of the Four Articles, of the Calixtines, who maintained that both the bread and the wine should be administered to the people during the Eucharist.

es and the craze for miracles. Like Dante, a hundred years before, he lamented the Donation of Constantine[31] as the basis of the false claim on the part of the pope for temporal power.[32] He scourged bishops, doctors [teachers of divinity], priests, and especially monks, who suck the blood of the poor by begging. He declared that human laws, fasts, feasts, processions and other matters had driven the commands of God into the background. He also declared that the sale of indulgences, the worship of relics, and miracles drew people from true piety. Finally he declared it his aim to help abolish all these accretions and to lead the Church back to its original simplicity. 'I believe', he prophesied, 'that all these above-named works of men, ordinances, and ceremonies will be utterly extirpated, cut up by the roots and cease, and that God alone will be exalted and his Word will abide forever, and the time is close at hand when these ordinances shall be abolished.'

Although Matěj z Janova did not openly combat the hierarchical system, yet he must be looked upon as a forerunner of Protestantism when we consider the spirit of his teaching. Among other things, he declared that the law of the Holy Ghost as seen in the Bible is enough for the government of the Church, and that all human ordinances and traditions should be abolished and the

---

[31] A forged Roman imperial decree by which Emperor Constantine the Great supposedly transferred authority over Rome and the western part of the Roman Empire to the Pope in the 4th century. However, it was probably composed in the 8th century. It was used, especially in the 13th century, to support the papacy's claims of political authority by the papacy.

[32] In his *Divina Commedia* [*Divine Comedy*], written in the early 14th century, Dante wrote of the Donation of Constantine: 'Ah, Constantine, how much evil was born, / not from your conversion, but from that donation / that the first wealthy pope received from you!'

Church led back to the simplicity of apostolic times. He asserted that the only condition for the salvation of man is to be born again of the Spirit by faith in Jesus Christ, and that this is the pure gift of grace on the part of God. Furthermore, in this faith every man has free access to God and to Jesus Christ, and the community of those who know and exercise this freedom—and they alone form the true Christian Church. The logical result of all these doctrines would be utterly to destroy the whole fabric of the hierarchical system, from the pope down to the humblest priest, to abolish forever all forms and ceremonies which stood between man and his God, and to reduce public worship to its simplest elements.

The influence of Matěj of Janov was very great. He gave to Hus the first impulse to his reforming movement, and his writings scattered far and wide over all Bohemia created a widespread desire for a change in religious matters.

Chapter 3

Early life and activity of Hus

When we consider the place occupied by Jan Hus in history, it is a source of the deepest regret that we possess so few details about his early life and the development of his religious consciousness. Biography—and especially autobiography—are among the most fascinating as well as most useful kinds of literature. What a loss to the world it would have been if Augustine had never written his *Confessions*! We have practically a complete knowledge of the external and internal life of Luther and others, but of the story of Jan Hus we know only the details of the last few years, which precede his death and martyrdom at Constance.

It is true that these years are the ones that are of most importance, for in them he accomplished the work, the effects of which will be felt as long as time shall last. It is likewise a matter of rejoicing that we have not only the testimony of friends, the reports of committees, and the decrees of the Council of Constance, but also a minute account of Hus's life in prison by Petr z Mladoňovic[33] [Peter of Mladoňovice], as well as a number of letters written by Hus himself.

Birth of Hus

Jan Hus was born on 6th July 1369, just forty-six years to the day before his death at Constance. Like Luther, he belonged to the common people, his parents being peasants. Their name is now unknown, for Hus took his name from the little market town of Husinec,[34] where he was born, or rather from the castle nearby called Hus.[35]

University education

Everything relating to Hus's childhood and early school life is either utterly unknown or based upon unreliable tradition. The earliest real information we have concerning him is his appearance at the University of Prague, where he studied under the most celebrated men of the day, among whom were Jan z Štěkně[36] [John of Štěkeň], Mikuláš z Litomyšle[37] [Nicholas of

---

[33] Pronounced Petr Zmladonyovits. Mladoňovice (pronounced Mladonyovitseh) is a village in southern Bohemia, near the border with Austria, situated 91 miles (147 km) from Prague.

[34] Prounounced Hoosinets. A small town in the South Bohemian region of the Czech Republic, near the borders of Germany and Austria.

[35] The Bohemian word 'hus' means a goose. He often alluded to this pun himself.

[36] Pronounced Yan Zshtyeknyeh. Štěkeň (pronounced Shtyekeny) lies approximately 60 miles (96 km) south of Prague.

[37] Pronounced Meekulash Zleetomeeshleh. Litomyšl is a cathedral town situated 85 miles (136 km) east of Prague in the Pardubice Region of eastern Bohemia.

Litomyšl], and Stanislav ze Znojma[38] [Stanislas of Znojmo]. In September 1393 Hus received the degree of Bachelor of Free Arts, in 1394 that of Bachelor of Theology, and in 1396 that of Master of Arts. As his ranking among those who graduated with him at this time was only about the middle, it indicates that his teachers did not regard him as a man of unusual ability.

Teacher at the university

In 1398, Hus appeared as a public teacher at the university, and in the following year, 1399, he defended certain propositions of Wycliffe, thus coming into contest for the first time with his colleagues.

At that time, the University of Prague was one of the greatest universities in the world, ranking with those of Paris, Bologna, and Oxford. In 1408 there were said to be as many as two hundred doctors, five hundred Bachelors of Arts, and thirty thousand students. All sciences then known were taught, every Master of Arts had the privilege at his own will of giving public and private lectures, and every student could attend what lectures he pleased. As Palacký says, this perfect freedom, both in hearing and in giving lectures, undoubtedly explains the extraordinary crowds of students that came to Prague from all parts of Europe.

We know from Hus's works that he made the most of his opportunities. His works show him to be a man of high scholarship, although by no means so able a thinker as Wycliffe, or so brilliant a philosophical debater as his younger contemporary,

---

[38] Pronounced Stanislaf Zeznoyma. Znojma is a town in southern Moravia, located 111 miles (179 km) southeast of Prague, close to the present border of Austria.

Jerome of Prague. Yet, although he was an eager student, he realised that learning is not everything. In one of his synodal sermons he declared:

> First of all we must learn that which is most necessary to salvation, that which stimulates us to love, for we should learn not for vainglory or curiosity, but to the edification of ourselves and our neighbour, and to the glory of our Lord Jesus Christ. There are some who wish to know, in order that they may be known of men, and that is degrading vanity. There are others who wish to know, for the sake of knowing, and that is curiosity. And there are still others who wish to know, in order to sell their knowledge for wealth and honour, and that is ignoble desire for gain. But there are likewise some who desire to know, in order to edify, and that is love, and still others who desire to know, in order to be edified themselves, and that is wisdom.

Although Hus was not a great scholar, yet his learning was broad and solid, as the reading of his books and the reports of his disputations [formal academic debates] abundantly show. He knew something of Greek, but less of Hebrew. However, he was thoroughly grounded in Latin, and at home in philosophy, especially Aristotle and Plato. As to his knowledge of Church history and the Church Fathers, his works give ample testimony of this, as they are full of quotations from Chrysostom, Origen, Jerome, Augustine, Peter Lombard, Thomas Aquinas, and others. At the Council of Constance he later showed himself to be no mean adversary of the great lights of the philosophical and theological world, especially Gerson[39] and Pierre d'Ailly.[40]

---

[39] Jean Charlier de Gerson (1363–1429) was the Chancellor of the University of Paris. He was an educator and reformer, and one of the most eminent theologians at the Council of Constance. Although he

At that early time Hus was still a devout adherent to the doctrines and even forms of the Church, for we are told how in 1393 he gave the last four groš[41] he had to his confessor, 'so that he had nothing more to eat than dry bread'. His life must have been blameless from his youth up, for his bitterest enemies never ventured to cast the least aspersion on his personal conduct. He himself, it is true, just before his death blamed himself for vanity, anger, and frivolous amusements. Hus wrote a letter to a certain Master Martin, showing his tender conscience. He wrote this before his departure from Bohemia, but he requested it should not be opened until Master Martin was assured that Hus must die.

> You have known my preaching and exhortations from your childhood; but I beseech you, by the mercy of our Lord, not to follow me in any of the vanities into which you have seen me fall. Know, alas, that before I became a priest I consumed a great deal of time in playing chess, and that in so doing I was often angry myself and provoked others to anger. I beg your prayers for this sin of mine and for my innumerable transgressions.

Hus must have been successful as a teacher, for not only was he supported in his later struggles by practically the whole body of students, but also we find him making rapid advancement in his

---

attempted to reform abuses in the Roman Catholic Church, he was one of the most prominent opponents of Hus at the Council.

[40] Pierre d'Ailly (1351–1420) was a French theologian, who preceded Gerson as Chancellor of the University of Paris. He attended the Council of Constance as the Cardinal of Cambrai.

[41] A groš (pronounced grosh) was a mediaeval Bohemian silver coin, literally 'a thick coin'. It was known in other countries as a groschen, and in English as a groat.

academic career. On 15ᵗʰ October 1401, he was elected Dean of the Philosophical Faculty, and a year later he became Rector of the whole university.[42] These facts in themselves should warn us not to go too far in denying to Hus (as some have done) the possession of a high degree of learning and administrative ability.

Scholasticism

One phase of Hus's education, which seems puerile to us today, was of vast importance at that time and exerted a baleful influence on his after career—namely, his system of philosophy. During the whole of the Middle Ages, philosophy and theology were one, and under the name of Scholasticism absorbed the attention of the brightest minds in the Church. As the dogmas of Christianity were absolutely true, and could be denied by none but heretics, the problem of philosophy was no longer to seek after truth, but to explain the dogmas of the Church, deduce their consequences, and show their harmony with human reason. Beginning with Scotus Erigena,[43] carried on by Anselm of Canterbury,[44] Pierre Abélard [Peter Abelard],[45] Lombard,[46]

---

[42] Tenure was for one year, and he was later appointed Rector for a second time, 1409–1410.

[43] John Scotus Erigena (or Eriugena) (c. 815–c. 877) was an Irish theologian and philosopher.

[44] Anselm of Canterbury (c. 1033–1109) was a theologian of the Catholic Church, who held the office of archbishop of Canterbury from 1093 to 1109. He wrote with a rational and philosophical approach, and this has led to him being known as the founder of Scholasticism.

[45] Pierre Abélard (1079–1142) was a French philosopher, theologian and logician.

[46] Pierre Lombard (c. 1096–1160), also known as Peter Lombard or Petrus Lombardus, was Bishop of Paris, and author of *The Four Books*

and others, Scholasticism reached its climax in Thomas Aquinas,[47] whose *Summa Theologiæ* became the official philosophy of the Church, a position that it nominally holds even today.

Scholasticism, however, early became split up into two great parties—the Realists and the Nominalists. The Realists declared that universals (*i.e.*, the characteristics or qualities of certain things) actually existed,[48] while the individuals that make up the world of phenomena are only a fleeting symbol or sign of their unchangeable and eternal prototypes. On the other hand, common sense tended to regard universals as mere notions of the mind—*i.e.*, a mere name, signs and abstractions, while the individuals alone are real. This branch of Scholasticism was called Nominalism.

The growing spread of Nominalism, especially through William of Occam,[49] led largely to the breaking down of the universal power of the Church, and was thus naturally allied to the doctrines of the Reformation. However, Nominalism was not the philosophical system of Hus, but it was that of his most distinguished adversaries at the Council of Constance, Gerson and d'Ailly.

---

of Sentences, which became the standard mediaeval textbook of theology.

[47] Thomas Aquinas (1225–1274), was an Italian Dominican friar and an immensely influential scholastic theologian.

[48] For example, suppose there are two chairs in a room, each of which is green. These two chairs both share the quality of 'chairness', as well as 'greenness' or the quality of being green.

[49] William of Occam (or Ockham) (*c.* 1287–1347) was an English Franciscan friar, philosopher and theologian.

At the time of Hus's appearance in the world of public life, the reigning system of philosophy, both in Paris and throughout Germany, was Nominalism. John Wycliffe, however, was a Realist, and it was through the study of his philosophical books, known in Bohemia as early as 1285, that Hus and many others became Realists. Wycliffe's book, *De Universalibus* [*Concerning Universals*] was for years a textbook in the University of Prague. Within a short time, Hus became an enthusiastic disciple of the English Reformer, but at first Hus regarded him merely as a philosopher. Yet the *odium philosophicum*[50] thus aroused against Wycliffe had much to do with Hus's death later.

From this we see that Hus first became prominent in public through his teaching on philosophy. The philosophical teachings of Realism had become very widespread in Bohemia. Hus was considered its chief exponent, and was followed by the vast majority of Bohemian youth. Among the scholars who at this time sided with him were Stanislav ze Znojma, Petr ze Znojma[51] [Peter of Znojmo], and Štěpán z Pálče[52] [Stephen Paletz], all of whom later became his bitterest enemies. Other scholars, who remained faithful to him, were Jerome of Prague, Mikuláš z Litomyšle, Jakoubek ze Stříbra, and Petr z Mladoňovic, who later wrote the account of Hus's life in the prisons of Constance. On the other side, however, a hostile party was ranged against him, consisting chiefly of foreigners.

---

[50] A Latin phrase which means 'philosophical hatred'. A term used to the often intense anger and hatred generated by disputes over philosophy.
[51] Pronounced Petr Zeznoyma.
[52] Pronounced Shtyepan Spaltsheh.

All these things form more or less important parts of the events which led Hus to his reforming efforts. However, they in themselves would have been of little influence had it not been for other events which soon took place.

Hus as an orator

Among the greatest gifts of Hus was that of public oratory. He developed a power in preaching which soon made him widely known, and so when the famous Bethlehem Chapel[53] in Prague was in need of a preacher in 1402 it was natural that those in charge should think of him.

The establishment of this most interesting institution was undoubtedly due to the influence of Matěj z Janova and Jan Milíč z Kroměříže. Two citizens of Prague—Hanušem z Mühlheimu[54] [John of Mülheim] and a merchant called Kříž[55]—conceived the idea of a place where the gospel could be heard by the people in their native tongue, and to this end they built at their own expense a chapel, to which they gave the name of Bethlehem Chapel. Among other things contained in its charter was the stipulation that sermons should be preached in the Bohemian language in the morning and afternoon of every Lord's Day and on holy days.

---

[53] Betlémská kaple in Czech. Founded in 1391, it could hold 3000 people. It was handed over to the Moravian Church in the early 17th century. However, due to the spread of the Counter-Reformation, the Jesuits obtained the building later that century. It fell into disrepair and was demolished in 1786. Most of the exterior survived, however, and the building was restored in the 20th century. The wall paintings and part of the pulpit date from Hus's time.
[54] Pronounced Hanooshem Zmulheimoo.
[55] Pronounced Krzheezh.

Bethlehem Chapel, Prague

Hus was the fourth person to be called to the office of preacher in the chapel. His success was extraordinary. In the words of Palacký:

The sermons preached during many years by this man in the Bethlehem Chapel of Old Prague were among the most important events of his time. Less coarse in his sermons than Konrád Waldhauser, less exaggerated in his views than Milíč, he did not affect his hearers so powerfully as his predecessors, and yet his success was far more lasting. He appealed especially to the common sense of his hearers, aroused their interest, taught and convinced them, and yet he was not lacking in impressiveness. Several attributes raised him far above his colleagues and contemporaries. Among these were keenness and clearness of his mind, the tact with which he penetrated to the very heart of a question, the ease with which he knew how to develop it before the eyes of all, the wide reading, especially in the Holy Scriptures, and the firmness and logic with which he proved a whole system of principles. To all this we may add the deep earnestness of his character, his devout spirit, a personal conduct in which even his enemies could find nothing to blame, a burning zeal for the moral elevation of the people, as well as for the reformation of the ecclesiastical conditions of his time. At the same time, he showed boldness and firmness, and a strange seeking after popularity and love of fame, which looked upon the martyr's crown as the highest goal of human life.

Not only were his sermons listened to by vast throngs of the lower classes, but also by the students and the aristocracy. Even the queen herself came to Bethlehem Chapel nearly every week, and she made Hus her personal confessor.

The sermons of Hus

We only know about his early sermons largely from hearsay, but we know their characteristic features on broad lines. They covered the whole field of Church doctrines, based on the Scripture that was laid down for the day. They exposed the hypocrisy and corruption of the lax clergy, and showed the contrast between the teachings of Christ as seen in the Gospels and the whole system of the Roman Catholic hierarchy. They boldly attacked the crying evils of the Church, such as the widespread sale of indulgences, and they unfavourably contrasted the entry of Christ into Jerusalem with the luxury of prelates and bishops.

The appointment of Hus to the position of preacher at Bethlehem Chapel was not only epoch-making for the Bohemian Reformation, but had the greatest possible influence on his own character. It was here that his eyes were first opened to see the whole truth as it is in Christ Jesus. In preparing for his sermons, he studied the Bible thoroughly, and more and more he realised how great the contrast was between the gospel and the Church of his own day. By means of the standard of the Scriptures, he could not help criticising the conduct of the clergy, from the pope down to the lowest priest, and he could not help seeing how much the claims of universal power on the part of the papacy were at variance with the statement of Christ, 'My kingdom is not of this world.' He thus laid the foundation of that unshakable principle, that the Bible alone is the only true code of the Christian life, a principle that was later to lead him to the stake.

Opposition of corrupt clergy

While his own character was being formed and while the common people heard him gladly, by his fierce onslaughts against the clergy he became the object of their bitter hatred. Yet, if he had not gone further than this, he would have suffered no harm. All Christendom at that time felt the scandal of the clergy and proclaimed the necessity of reform. Hus was no more outspoken in his scourging of the corruptions of the Church than Gerson and d'Ailly, who afterwards did so much to destroy him at the Council of Constance. Indeed, one of the chief reasons for calling that council itself was for the express purpose of reforming the clergy.

In Prague itself, Hus was supported by those highest in authority, both in Church and State. King Václav was favourable to him, and Archbishop Zbyněk[56] ordered him to report to him all cases of corruption among the clergy that might come under his notice. In addition, Zbyněk made him synodal preacher. How-

---

[56] Zbyněk Zajíc z Hazmburka (pronounced Zbeenyek Zayeets. Z-hazmburka) [Zbyněk Zajíc of Hazmburk or of Hasenburg] (c. 1376–1411). He was a military adviser to Vacláv IV. Although he was not a priest, he was appointed as Archbishop of Prague in 1403. Zbyněk was initially favourable to Hus. Pressure from the Pope and clergy led to him changing his attitude to Hus, however.

ever, several things soon led to an increase of hatred against Hus, and tended to estrange from him many who had hitherto been his friends. This finally led to a state of affairs in which retraction or martyrdom were the only alternatives.

The 'miracle' of Wilsnack

The first point of conflict was the so-called miracle of Wilsnack. In 1383, a raid by a robber baron destroyed a church in the town of Wilsnack, in Brandenburg, Germany. In a cavity of a stone altar, which had been left partly standing, three wafers had been found, coloured red as if with blood. It was declared by the priests that this was the blood of Christ.

The fame of this supposed miracle was spread everywhere throughout all Europe. Wilsnack became a place of pilgrimage, visited by great crowds from Hungary, Poland, and even the Scandinavian countries of the distant north. A shrewd suspicion was raised that not all was right, and that the priests of Wilsnack had used tricks and falsehood in order to encourage the pilgrimages that were so profitable to them.

Archbishop Zbyněk forbade his own people to take part in these pilgrimages, and appointed a committee of three men to inquire into the matter. Among them was Jan Hus, to whose influence we may largely ascribe a report that was adverse to the genuineness of the supposed miracles. It was on this occasion that he wrote his tract, *De Omni Sanguine Christi Glorificato* [*Concerning the whole blood of Christ glorified*]. In this, although he remained perfectly in line with the Roman Catholic doctrine of transubstantiation, he yet showed himself utterly opposed to the superstitions and frauds so intimately connected with the worship of relics and the exploitation of miracles.

The report of the committee showed that the so-called miracles were fraudulent. It was said that the foot of a boy had been healed; 'We found that his foot was worse than before.' Two blind women were said to have received their sight; 'They confessed before many people, before us and the notary, that they had never been blind, although suffering from poor sight.' A citizen of Prague, whose hand was withered, offered at Wilsnack a silver hand. Wishing to know what the priest would say about this hand, he remained there three days. Then he heard the priest in his own presence say: 'Hear, children, about a new miracle. Behold, a citizen of Prague has been cured of a withered hand through the blood of Christ. In witness of this he has brought this silver hand as an offering.' Then the citizen, who was among the congregation, raised his hand and said, 'See, here is my hand, withered as before.'

All this made a tremendous stir throughout the land. If the miracles of Wilsnack were frauds, what about all the others? The whole subject of relics and miracles was in danger of being brought into indifference and contempt, and an unfailing source of power and financial profit would be lost. No wonder that Hus's prominence in this affair increased the hatred that his unsparing denunciation of the clergy had already brought upon him. Years after he was falsely accused of 'heresy' on the question of transubstantiation, largely owing to his activity in the affair of Wilsnack.

The spread of Wycliffe's doctrines

Hus's article *De Omni Sanguine* marked his first appearance before the world as a writer and reformer. Another event that had the deepest influence, both on the intellectual and religious development of Hus himself and on the entire reforming movement, was the spread of Wycliffe's doctrines in Bohemia. As previously mentioned, several of his books had been known before 1385. They were now read with intense enthusiasm at the University of Prague, and counted among their adherents some of the most distinguished men of the day, among them Mikuláš z Litomyšle, Stanislav ze Znojma, Štěpán z Pálče, Jan Hus, and Jerome of Prague.

Jerome, who was to have his name indissolubly joined to that of Hus by suffering the same death (and for the same cause) at Constance, had done much for the study of Wycliffe in Bohemia. Some years younger than Hus, born to a noble family of Prague, endowed with keen intellect and extraordinary oratorical powers, he had studied in nearly all the universities of Europe, among them Heidelberg, Cologne, Oxford, and Paris. He received the degree of Master of Arts at Paris. On his return from Oxford, he had brought back a number of Wycliffe's books, which were previously unknown to his countrymen. We have his own words for this when, before the Council of Constance, he said, 'I confess that when I was still a youth, full of love for learning, I went to England, and hearing the fame of Wycliffe, how that he was a man of fine, keen, and extraordinary intellect, I made copies of his *Dialogue* and *Trialogue* and brought them back to Prague.'

Through the efforts of Hus and Jerome, supported by the others mentioned above, an extraordinary impetus was given to the study of Wycliffe's doctrines at the university. Archbishop Zbyněk was somewhat indifferent at first. However, he became alarmed when he received a letter from the Archbishop of Canterbury to the effect that not only the English Church, but also the University of Oxford had condemned the works of Wycliffe, but by then it was too late to stem the tide.

There is no doubt that, just as the Wilsnack affair gave the first impetus to an open break between Hus and the hierarchy, so the whole Wycliffe movement gave an additional and still more powerful impulse to it. It furnished to his enemies what they did not have before—a weapon in the form of accusations of heresy. An untiring and unremitting effort was made to fasten the whole condemnation attached to the name of Wycliffe upon Hus himself. In all attacks made against Hus, from now on until the last tragic episode at Constance, the two names were inextricably bound together.

Papal opposition to Wycliffe in Bohemia

The issues had now been joined. Instigated by the prelates of Prague, Pope Innocent VII ordered Archbishop Zbyněk to take immediate and drastic measures to destroy Wycliffe's teaching in Bohemia. In spite of the earnest efforts of such men as Hus and Stanislav ze Znojma, a decree was passed on 28th May 1403. It was to the effect that henceforth no member of the university should publicly or privately teach or help spread the doctrines contained in the twenty-four articles of Wycliffe, condemned by the London Council in 1382, or in the additional twenty-one articles now extracted from Wycliffe's works by a German master of theology, John Hübner.

This act of condemnation, as Palacký says, was the first great public act which bore witness to the deep division in the views of Hus's contemporaries concerning the Christian Church and its teachings. One consequence of all these things was an increased bitterness against Hus, who never for a moment ceased his sermons against ecclesiastical corruptions. In spite of the archbishop's friendly feelings towards him, Zbyněk was forced to deprive Hus of his position as synodal preacher.

The Western Schism

All these merely local struggles were soon overshadowed by events of worldwide importance, however. The one great burning question in all Christendom was now the great schism, which scandalised all classes and did more to undermine the power of the papacy in the minds of the people than any other thing.

The roots of the Western Schism run back to the times of Philippe IV of France and Pope Boniface VIII. After the death of that celebrated usurper of the papal chair, who 'came in like a fox, ruled like a lion, and died like a dog', Benedict XI ruled the Church for the short period of eight months. Then, in 1305, Bertrand de Got, Archbishop of Bordeaux, made a shameful bargain with Philippe IV, by which he was elected pope under the title of Clement V. One of the conditions of his election was that he should remove the seat of the papacy from Rome to France.

Thus began the famous 'Babylonian Captivity' of the papacy, during which Avignon and not Rome was the centre of the Christian Church.[57] During all these years, the French popes

---

[57] Conflict between the Papacy and the French crown led to the Avignon Papacy. During the period from 1309 to 1377, seven successive popes resided in the French city of Avignon (then in the Kingdom of Arles, part of the Holy Roman Empire) rather than in Rome. The Avignon Papacy was supported by France, Spain and Scotland, whereas

were little more than the tools of the King of France, and Avignon itself became a sink of corruption, both moral and political, a corruption that spread through all lands.

Papal palace, Avignon
(Photograph attribution: Jean-Marc Rosier, www.rosier.pro)

During the years that followed, a stronger and stronger desire arose within the Church for the pope's return to Rome. The Italian humanist,[58] Petrarch, in a letter to Pope Urban V, elected in 1362, used all his eloquence in urging him to transfer his seat to Rome, even going so far as to assure the pleasure-loving cardinals that Italy would afford them as good wines as the South

---

the Roman Papacy was supported by most of Italy, Germany and England.

[58] Renaissance Humanism consisted of the study of classical antiquity. The movement began in Italy and then spread across Western Europe in the 14th, 15th and 16th centuries. Humanists wished to create a citizenry able to speak and write with the eloquence and clarity of the ancient Greeks and Romans. They envisaged that this would enable people to engage more effectively in the civic life of their communities and would persuade others to virtuous and prudent actions. This was to be accomplished through the study of the *studia humanitatis* (Latin: the study of humanity), today known as the humanities—grammar, rhetoric, history, poetry, and moral philosophy.

of France. In a similar manner, the Italian mystic, Catherine of Siena, called on his successor, Gregory XI, to accomplish this object.

Gregory went to Rome in 1376, accompanied by a number of his cardinals, but he died soon after. His death was the signal of the most bitter quarrels between the cardinals of France and those of Italy. After many contests and intrigues, the cardinals who were at Rome elected Urban VI, a Neapolitan. However, not long after, many of those who opposed the election of an Italian pope went to Avignon and protested against the validity of Urban's election, declaring that it had been made under duress. Next they went to Fondi, a town halfway between Rome and Naples, where they could feel safe from all interference, and elected Robert de Genève, who took the name of Clement VII. The appointment of this first antipope was the beginning of the great schism in the Western Church, which, as Neander says, 'was one of the most important of the links in the chain of events which contributed to the overthrow of the papal absolutism of the Middle Ages, and to prepare for the great reaction of the Christian mind which took place in the sixteenth century'.

This scandalous state of affairs divided all Christendom. One party, headed by France (and including Scotland), upheld Clement VII, whereas the other—including Germany, Hungary, Poland, Bohemia and England—followed Urban VI. As the intrigue and corruption caused by the schism grew progressively more scandalous, a third party remained neutral, and openly declared that the only deliverance for the Church was through a general Ecumenical Council.

This desire culminated in the Council of Pisa in 1409, which met for two chief reasons: first, to reform the corruption of the clergy, and second, to put an end to the schism.[59] At this time, Benedict XIII was antipope at Avignon and Gregory XII the 'official' pope at Rome. The Pisan Council declared these men schismatics and heretics, deposed them from all their ecclesiastical dignities, and after that proceeded to elect a third rival pope, the Archbishop of Milan, who took the name of Alexander V.[60] He lived only a short time, and was followed by one of the most corrupt and execrable characters in Church history, Baldassare Cossa. This man was stained with all manner of vice, and was even accused of having killed one of his predecessors by poison. In 1410, Cossa mounted the papal throne under the name of John XXIII.

Alas for the expectations of those who had hoped so much from the Council of Pisa! Matters became worse than ever. As soon as he was elected, Alexander dissolved the Council without keeping his promise to reform the clergy. Neither Benedict XIII nor Gregory XII would resign, and they were still supported by many of their princely adherents. Thus the election of another pope had only added a new division of parties, and the schism now became more scandalous than ever.

---

[59] The Council of Pisa was an 'unrecognised' Ecumenical Council of the Roman Catholic Church.
[60] The Western Schism led eventually to two competing lines of antipopes: the Avignon line (as Clement VII took up residence in Avignon) and the Pisan one. The Council of Pisa elected antipope Alexander V as a third claimant to the papacy. In May 1415, the Council of Constance deposed the second and final Pisan antipope, John XXIII, and this brought the Pisan papacy to an end.

Bohemian reaction to the Western Schism

In Bohemia, King Václav had promised to keep neutral between the two popes, Benedict and Gregory, and had urged the prelates and the University of Prague likewise to remain neutral, just as the University and prelates of Paris had done. However, Archbishop Zbyněk and the German branch of the University refused to give up their allegiance to Pope Gregory XII. Hus and the Bohemian members of the University openly declared in favour of the king's views, and advocated a neutral attitude about the schism. This was the beginning of the quarrel between Hus and Zbyněk, who hitherto had been favourably inclined to him, and had approved of his efforts in the way of reform. It also led to the first Church censure pronounced against Hus. This came in the form of an order from the archbishop to stop preaching, an order that Hus refused to obey.

German secession from the University of Prague

Closely connected with this question of neutrality was the notable secession of the German members of the University of Prague, who followed the lead of Archbishop Zbyněk and refused to give up their allegiance to Gregory XII, in spite of all efforts on the part of King Václav to induce them to do so. This called attention anew to a question which had been agitated before, and in which patriotic fervour was to join hands with religious feelings. Hus, who was an ardent patriot, as well as reformer, took a leading part in these events. Later, he was wrongfully accused of having been the chief instigator of the movement.

We have already seen that of the four 'nations' constituting the University, three (the Bavarian, Saxon and Polish) were practically composed of Germans. The Polish 'nation', in spite of its name, consisted chiefly of German-speaking groups—Silesians, Pomeranians and Prussians. These German groups invariably voted as one body against the Bohemians, whom they thus outnumbered three to one. This they did now (1409) in standing up for Gregory XII, in spite of the fact that a majority of the cardinals, the Universities of Paris, Bologna, and Oxford, and most of the Christian rulers of the world had given him up.

There was a certain element of treason in this conduct on the part of the German 'nations' of the University, inasmuch as Pope Gregory supported Ruprecht von der Pfalz [Rupert, Count Palatine], the rival of King Václav IV, as candidate for the crown of the Holy Roman Empire. The influential position of the Germans had long been a painful point for the Bohemians. After the middle of the 14th century, Karel IV had promoted German immigration to Bohemia and large numbers moved there. Since then, they had become predominant, not only in the University, where their three 'nation' votes gave them a practical monopoly, but in the city of Prague as well.

As the German 'nations' were faithful supporters of the Roman Catholic Church, they were naturally bitter opponents of Hus and his reforming ideas. On the other hand, the great body of Bohemians were his warm supporters. As long as the Germans retained their influential position in Prague, Hus could do little more than stir up strife, but as soon as they left, all Bohemia, except the higher clergy, became a unit in his favour. Hence we see that a matter, that seemed merely a question of local university interest at first sight, was destined to play an important role in shaping the destiny of the Hussite movement.

The question of votes on the part of the four 'nations' now had a practical interest. The king sent a commission to the University of Paris to inquire into the method of voting in vogue there. When he received the information he sought, he immediately made a decree to the effect that hereafter the native-born Bohemian 'nation' in all decrees and university business should have three votes, whereas the three foreign 'nations' should have but one between them. This mandate, published on 18th January 1409, is known as the Decree of Kutná Hora. It was a terrible blow to the Germans, who at once saw that it meant the loss forever of their influence in shaping the business and teachings of the University. It meant likewise the utter loss of prestige for the University of Prague as a cosmopolitan institution. Up to this time, it had been regarded as the equal in learning and number of students to the sister universities of Oxford and Paris, but it was soon to sink to the level of a national school only.

The three German 'nations'—the Saxon, Bavarian, and Polish—were angry and indignant. On 6th February 1409, they handed in to the king a respectful, though energetic, protest against the royal decree. When they found they could expect no help from him, they met together on 16th February, and swore one to the other that they would sooner leave the country than accept the new order of things.

There was a paralysis in the management of university affairs in the midst of all these agitations. In consequence, the king himself appointed a rector of the University and a dean of the Philosophical Faculty, both of them Bohemians. Immediately the German students and masters, carrying out their oath, began to leave Prague in crowds, some on foot, some on horseback, and some in carriages. It is said that as many as two thousand left the city in one day. Practically no students remained at Prague except Bohemians. The German universities gained from this secession, however. Not only did student numbers increase at the existing German universities, but a new university, that of Leipzig, was founded by the Elector of Saxony this same year of 1409, and was largely composed of students who had left the Bohemian capital. This notable secession of German students from Prague was an event laden with consequences to Germany and Bohemia in general, and to Hus and the Hussite movement in particular.

Chapter 4

Hus and the Roman Catholic hierarchy

For the moment, the new turn of affairs seemed favourable to King Václav IV and Hus. The Council of Pisa had recognised Václav as the regular King of the Romans, and had ignored the claims of Ruprecht von der Pfalz. Hus himself was appointed court preacher.

Reorganisation of the University of Prague

The University of Prague was reorganised on a new basis, and as the Germans had been the chief opponents of the Wycliffe party, the latter now rose to the leading role in the teachings of that institution. The king, and the nobility for the most part, were on their side; only Archbishop Zbyněk and the higher clergy were against them. Hus seemed now to have reached the climax of his glory and influence. He was famous throughout the land. As an evidence of his prominence, we may mention his election in October 1409 to be the first rector of the reorganised university.

This apparent prosperity, however, lasted only a short time. Hus's enemies were still active. At first they were apparently unsuccessful in their attempts to destroy him. But from now on they increased their efforts. Little by little, and aided by outward

events, and by Hus's own fearlessness in championing what he
thought was right and in scourging the injustice and unrighteousness on the part of the pope, they brought on the final catastrophe of 1415.

Papal Bull against Wycliffe's teaching

Archbishop Zbyněk had remained loyal to Pope Gregory XII
during the struggle on the question of neutrality about the rival
popes. Zbyněk now suddenly turned about and declared in favour of Alexander V, the new antipope elected by the Council
of Pisa in June 1409. This action was ominous for Hus and the
Wycliffe party, for very soon, in December 1409, Zbyněk obtained a bull from the new pope.[61] This authorised him to root
out all 'heresy' in his diocese, to prevent at all hazards the spread
of Wycliffe's doctrines, and to require all those who possessed
copies of his writings to deliver them up. The bull also forbade
all preaching except in places privileged by the Church.

This bull at once relit the slumbering fires of contest. Hus accused the archbishop of slandering Bohemia and appealed to the
pope, but in vain. He was cited to Rome to give account of himself and his teaching at the papal court. The death of Alexander V, a short time after this in May 1410, did not affect the
condition of affairs, for his successor, the antipope John XXIII,
continued the policy of uncompromising hostility to Hus.

In Prague itself, on 16th June 1410, the Synod, dominated by the
anti-Hus party, declared Wycliffe's books to be heretical, and
ordered all copies in Prague to be gathered up and publicly

---

[61] A papal bull is a decree issued by the pope. The name is derived
from the official papal lead seal (Latin: *bulla*) which authenticates the
document.

burned. In spite of the fact that the vast majority of the members of the university were followers of Hus, most of them were obedient to this decree, and handed in the copies of Wycliffe they possessed.

Decree against preaching in private chapels

Still more radical, however, was the decree forbidding all preaching in private chapels. This order struck Hus in his most vulnerable spot. Until this point he had not been openly disobedient to the highest ecclesiastical authorities, and in all questions that were discussed he had made an appeal directly to the pope, as an obedient and respectful son of the Church. If, however, he now should remain obedient and give up his preaching at Bethlehem Chapel, he would be completely silenced. He could not conscientiously comply with this, for it seemed to him that his duty to God was greater than that to any man, even the pope himself. From now on Hus was placed in a position of contumacy, not merely against the local archbishop, but against the Church of Rome itself.

Nine days later, on 25th June 1410, he gathered his friends in the Bethlehem Chapel and had a true account of the whole matter drawn up by a public notary. In the name of the university and practically all Bohemia, nobles, cities and towns, he sent a petition to John XXIII, begging him to issue an injunction to stop the archbishop from burning Wycliffe's books, and to prevent him prohibiting preaching in the private chapels. During all this time, however, Hus never ceased to preach for a single day. In a similar manner the whole university, doctors, masters and students (except a few who supported the archbishop) begged the king not to allow the burning of Wycliffe's books. Immediately the king ordered Zbyněk to suspend action until he, the king, could examine the question thoroughly.

In spite of Hus's appeal to the pope and the king's order, Zbyněk, weary of the delay, proceeded to carry out the decree of the Synod. On 16th July, the archbishop gathered the prelates and clergy together, surrounded by armed men. The books of Wycliffe were piled up, and whilst they sang the *Te Deum Laudamus*,[62] he committed the books to the flames. At the same time, the bells of all the churches in Prague announced to all the people what had been done.

Excommunication of Hus

Two days after burning Wycliffe's books, on 18th July, Zbyněk pronounced the ban of the Church over Hus and all his friends.

All these events produced the greatest commotion, not only among the students, but also among the great body of the people. The whole city was split into two hostile factions, who not only mutually insulted each other by means of songs and parodies, but they soon came to acts of violence. At one time, the archbishop himself was forced to retire from the cathedral while celebrating mass. At another time, when a priest attempted to proclaim from his pulpit the ban over Hus, six men with drawn swords attacked and nearly killed him.

The king made a vain attempt to allay the storm thus aroused. On the one hand, he forbade on pain of death the singing of satirical songs, and on the other hand, he ordered the archbishop to pay the owners of the books he had burnt. When Zbyněk

---

[62] An ancient hymn, whose title is from the opening words. In English, the title is *Thee, O God, we praise.*

refused to obey, King Václav gave orders to stop the payment of the salary of all those connected with burning the books.

Hus defies excommunication

Thus affairs stood for some time in a state of suspense. Hus and his followers were hopeful of final victory, as they were confident of the support of the nobility, magistrates, the common people, and even the king and queen. Hus continued to preach at Bethlehem Chapel, which was filled by enormous crowds. He became more and more bold, and carried the audience with him. Once when he spoke of having appealed to the pope, he asked his hearers, 'Will you stand by me?' and the whole vast congregation cried out, 'Yes, we will stand by you.'

They soon found, however, that nothing was to be hoped for from the pope. On 25th August 1410, John XXIII returned the appeal of Hus, confirmed the bull of his predecessor, Alexander V, requested the archbishop to continue the measures already taken, and ordered Hus to appear at the papal court within a specified time, there to give an account of himself. The publication of this decree resulted in new disorders. The king himself had no desire to support the hierarchy by force and was favourably inclined to Hus. Václav wrote to the pope, demanding among other things that the accusation against Hus should be withdrawn, and that Bethlehem Chapel should be restored to its rights.

This appeal was in vain too, for on 15th March 1411, the ban against Hus was proclaimed in all the churches of Prague except two, where the priests refused to read it. As this excommunication had no effect, Archbishop Zbyněk laid the whole city of

Prague under interdict. This meant that no services could take place in any church.

The extraordinary power and influence of Hus was never more apparent than at this crisis. Although the whole weight of ecclesiastical censure, the curse of the pope himself, had been directed against him, it did not shake the loyalty of his friends. Things remained much as before; ban and interdict were ignored. In many of the churches, services went on as usual, and Hus continued his sermons at Bethlehem Chapel.

The king proposes reconciliation

Thus the cleft between the people and the clergy grew wider and wider, and the only way of bringing about reconciliation was for both parties to show something of a spirit of compromise.

The king formed a plan, by which both Hus and Zbyněk should promise to abide by the decision of a committee of arbitrators appointed by the king. On 6th July 1411, the report of the committee was made public. Among other things, it recommended that the whole matter under discussion should be taken out of the hands of the pope, and settled in Bohemia itself. It also recommended that the archbishop should be asked to sign a document addressed to the pope, to the effect that in the course of his investigations he had not found any heresy, in either Bohemia or Moravia. Furthermore, the archbishop would state that he had come to a complete understanding with Hus and the university through the mediation of the king, and that he therefore requested John XXIII to recall the censure on Hus, and especially the command to appear before the papal Curia. On the other side, Hus was to agree to take certain similar steps towards bringing to an end the contest between them.

It seemed for a time as if finally a reconciliation, or at least a compromise, was at hand. At the last moment, however, the archbishop failed them. He left Prague secretly, sending word to the king that since he could not obtain an impartial hearing in Bohemia he had gone to King Václav's younger half-brother Zikmund Lucemburský[63] [Sigismund of Luxembourg], King of Hungary.

Death of Archbishop Zbyněk

This journey was fatal to Archbishop Zbyněk. He fell sick not long after he had crossed the frontiers of Moravia, and died at Prešpurk[64] in Hungary on 28th September 1411. His body was brought back to Prague, and buried amid general expressions of sorrow, for even his enemies had never denied him the credit of a good life and a well-meaning heart. Hus himself had never concealed his respect for his character.

Papal indulgences

After the death of Zbyněk, a temporary truce took place between Hus and his opponents. The new archbishop, Albík z Uničova[65] [Albert of Uničov], was almost twenty years older than Zbyněk, and he was by no means the man to continue the aggressive policy of his predecessor. Had it not been for new events—or rather if Hus had not found new fields for his reforming zeal—it is probable that the whole storm might have ended in peace and quiet. However, it led to a new outburst of

---

[63] Pronounced Zikmoont Lootsemboorskee.
[64] Pronounced Preshpoork. Whereas this was in Hungary in Hus's time, this city is now Bratislava, the capital of Slovakia.
[65] Pronounced Albeek Zoonitshova.

hate and bitterness against Hus, which would end in his death at the stake.

The cause of this new uproar was the arrival in Bohemia of Václav Tiem[66] [Wenceslaus Tiem], commissioned by the Pisan antipope John XIII to preach a crusade against King Ladislaus of Naples, and to sell indulgences for that purpose.

We have seen how the Council of Pisa had failed to abolish the Western Schism, and had only succeeded in adding to the general disgust by electing a third pope, John XXIII. It is true that most of the rulers of Europe had abandoned the Avignon antipope Benedict XIII and the 'official' Roman pope Gregory XII, yet some remained faithful to them. Among those who still supported Gregory was Ladislaus of Naples, who had driven John XXIII from Rome, after he had gone there from Bologna.

This action roused to a fury all the evil passions of John XXIII. He issued a bull of excommunication against Ladislaus, and ordered a crusade to be preached against him in all lands that acknowledged his own ecclesiastical authority. He also promised an indulgence to all the faithful, who should either fight in person or furnish money towards carrying on the war. This was the same indulgence as had previously been promised to all those who took part in the crusades against the pagans.

In May 1412, the papal legate, Václav Tiem, came to Prague to conduct the sale of John XXIII's indulgences in Bohemia, and the business was soon in full sway as the king and archbishop made no objections. The agents of Tiem appeared in the marketplaces, each time accompanied by drummers, and they invit-

---

[66] Pronounced Vatslaf Teem.

ed the people to contribute to the expenses of the pope in his war against Ladislaus, either with money or goods. Three moneyboxes were placed in the three principal churches of Prague. Great crowds gathered around, and a lively business was carried on.

Hus protests against the sale of indulgences

The whole affair created a great stir among the people, however. Hus himself could not restrain his indignation. He announced, by means of placards posted on the walls throughout the city, that a debate would be held on 7th June, on the subject, 'Whether according to the laws of Christ it was for the honour of God, the well-being of Christian people, and the best interests of the kingdom, for the followers of Christ to obey the commands of the pope in the matter of his crusade against Ladislaus.'

This debate promised to reopen the old contest between Hus and the hierarchy, and so the Theological Faculty of the University pleaded with the archbishop to forbid the debate being staged. In spite of this, however, the debate took place amid the greatest excitement.

Hus boldly declared that temporal rulers had the right to carry on wars, but that neither the pope nor bishops were ever justified in wielding the sword in the name of the Church. Christ himself had disapproved of using violence when he was betrayed by Judas, and he had healed the ear of the servant of the high priest, wounded by one of his followers. He had prayed for those who had persecuted him: 'Father, forgive them, for they know not what they do.' Hus maintained that, if the pope wished to overcome his enemies, he should pray for them as

Christ did; then the Lord would give him wisdom, so that his enemies could not hold out any longer against him.

Hus especially scourged the whole system of selling indulgences as being utterly at variance with the spirit of Christ and the teaching of the gospel. He maintained that the power of the priest to forgive sins rested only on repentance and contrition on the part of the guilty person. If it were based on the payment of money or property, it was simony, pure and simple, for had not the Saviour said, 'Freely ye have received, freely give'? The same thing applied to the pope, and the assertion made by some that the pope was infallible Hus declared to be not only false, but also sacrilegious, for this would make the pope equal to Christ himself. It goes without saying that these bold statements were not received without strenuous opposition on the part of the adherents of the hierarchy.

Although Hus was the leader in this debate, owing to his prominent position as the head of his party, yet the honours of the day were not accorded to him, but to Jerome of Prague. In a fiery and eloquent speech, Jerome so worked on the feelings of his hearers that he was given an ovation and was accompanied to his house by the enthusiastic student body.

Burning of papal Bulls

The debate was followed by an event that tended to still more increase the hatred between the two parties. A number of university men, among them Jerome, organised a parody of the scene two years before, when the books of Wycliffe had been publicly burnt. A magnificent procession was instituted, in the midst of which two courtesans sat on a wagon, each with one of the pope's bulls hanging from her neck by means of ribbons, while before and behind them marched a great crowd of men armed with swords and clubs. Pausing for a time in front of the archbishop's palace, they proceeded to the marketplace in the New Town,[67] where a funeral pyre was erected, on which the papal bulls were burnt.

Martyrdom of three young men

King Václav allowed this public disturbance to go unpunished, but at the same time he published a decree against any further insult to the pope or opposition to the Bull of Indulgences, on pain of death.

Nevertheless, the disturbances still went on. In three different churches, when the preacher defended the indulgences, three young men, apparently having agreed beforehand, cried out aloud, 'You lie! We have heard from Master Hus how all that is false.' They were thrown out of church, flogged, and dragged before the magistrates. The magistrates subjected the three young men to torture, and when they could not be forced to yield, they were sentenced to death.

The whole city was in an uproar. Hus felt it his duty to make an effort to rescue the unfortunate men. Followed by a great crowd of students and a number of university masters, he went to the Old Town Hall.[68] When he was admitted to the presence of the Senate, he begged earnestly for the lives of the prisoners. 'If anyone is guilty,' he said, 'it is I. I have done it. I and all these who

---

[67] Karel IV founded the New Town (Czech: Nové Město, pronounced Noveh Myesto) in 1348. It lay just outside the city walls to the east and south of the Old Town (Czech: Staré Město, pronounced Stareh Myesto) and is now an integral part of Prague.

[68] Czech: Staroměstská radnice (pronounced Staromyestska radnitseh).

are with me are ready to bear the same punishment.' The magistrates were alarmed at this demonstration of support, and promised that no blood should be shed. Hus then calmed the crowd,
which rapidly dispersed. In the meantime, the young men were
secretly hurried away and beheaded. This treacherous and cruel
act raised the public excitement to its highest point. A woman
brought clean linen cloths to shroud the bodies, which were
carried in procession to the Bethlehem Chapel, where, with the
assistance of Hus, they were solemnly buried. Henceforth the
three young men were looked upon by the Hussites as martyrs,
and Bethlehem Chapel was mockingly dubbed by their adversaries as the 'Chapel of the Three Saints'.

Second excommunication of Hus

The members of the anti-Hus party were driven to desperation
by all these events. They sent a message to Pope John XXIII,
calling his attention to the fact that for more than two years Hus
had been under the ban of the Church. During this time, he had
continued to teach the doctrines of Wycliffe, and now he was
bitterly opposing the preaching of the crusades against Ladislaus
and the sale of indulgences. Furthermore, his writings on this
subject had been scattered far and wide throughout Bohemia,
Moravia, Hungary and Poland. This message was communicated
to Pope John through the agent of the Prague clergy at Rome,
Michal z Brodu[69] [Michael of Deutschbrod[70]], better known un-

---

[69] Pronounced Michal Zbrodoo.
[70] Deutschbrod was the German name for the Bohemian town of
Německý Brod (pronounced Nyemetskee Brot). After World War II
and the expulsion of Germans from Czechoslovakia, it was renamed
Havlíčkův Brod (pronounced Havleetshkoov Brot).

der the name of Michal de Causis.[71] He was destined to be one of the chief instruments of the condemnation and execution of Hus at the Council of Constance.

The pope at once saw the seriousness of the situation, and commissioned Cardinal Peter St Angelo to proceed against Hus with the utmost severity. He further ordered the ban of excommunication to be proclaimed in all the churches of Prague. If Hus should still remain obstinate for twenty days, the curse of the Church should be laid upon him on 'Sundays' and holy days, in all the churches, amid the ringing of bells and extinguishing of candles. Under the penalty of excommunication, no faithful member of the Church should have anything to do with him, and should not give him food, drink or shelter. Wherever he should appear, divine service should cease at once, and if he should die, no one should give him Christian burial. In addition, other decrees ordered the faithful to seize the person of Hus and to deliver him up to the Archbishop of Prague or the Bishop of Litomyšl, and to see to it that Bethlehem Chapel should be razed to the ground.

This seemed to produce an effect at last. The magistrates of the Old Town, for the most part Germans and enemies of Hus, authorised a great crowd of men to proceed to Bethlehem Chapel, where Hus was preaching, for the purpose of driving out the congregation, taking Hus himself prisoner, and destroying the chapel. However, they met with such a firm resistance on the

---

[71] He was parish priest of St Adalbertus in Prague and Václav entrusted him with money to repair silver mines. Michal absconded with the money and went to Rome. He was later appointed 'Advocate in matters of faith' (Latin: *procurator de causis fidei*) by the Pisan antipope John XXIII and was therefore generally known as Michal de Causis.

part of Hus's friends, that they were forced to depart again with their object unaccomplished.

Defection of former friends

The papal ban served to strengthen the loyalty of Hus's friends. Nevertheless, it was a crisis in which the weak and cowardly were to be separated from the brave and true. A number of those, who had been on Hus's side in the question of Wycliffe's teaching, now became frightened and left him. Among them were Stanislav ze Znojma, Petr ze Znojma, and Štěpán z Pálče. Indeed, it was to these men that Hus chiefly owed his training in philosophy—as the popular genealogy had put it, 'Stanislav begat Petr, Petr begat Štěpán, and Štěpán begat Hus.'

All these men became his bitterest enemies, especially Štěpán z Pálče, who, with Michal de Causis, led the hostile party at Constance, and left no stone unturned to bring about the condemnation of his former friend. Of Štěpán, Hus wrote in 1413: 'He was once my closest friend and companion: now he has become my most hateful opponent.' There is a certain pathos in this breaking up of a friendship of many years' standing—on the side of Štěpán, the motive was fear; on the side of Hus, it was love of truth. Štěpán completely reversed his former attitude to Wycliffe, and now preached a sermon in which he called him a dangerous heretic. Immediately after this, Hus wrote in 1413, 'I said to him, and I have not spoken to him since, "My friend is Páleč, and my friend is likewise the truth; between these two, duty bids me to prefer the truth."'

On the other hand, Hus was cheered by the loyalty of many distinguished men, among them Jerome of Prague (who was destined to follow him to the stake at Constance), Jakoubek ze

Stříbra, who was the leader of the discussions on the administration of the communion in two kinds to the laity, thus giving rise later to the party of the Calixtines, and Jan z Jesenice[72] [John of Jessinic], who became the head of the reforming movement after the death of Hus.

Hus leaves Prague

In the meantime, however, the interdict over the city of Prague remained in force because of the presence of Hus. No services were held, no baptisms or marriages could be celebrated, nor could the dead be buried according to the rites of the 'Holy Church'. The seriousness of this state of affairs led the king to ask Hus to leave the city voluntarily. This he did in December 1412, not without many misgivings as to whether his real duty was to go or to stay.

---

[72] Pronounced Yan Zyeseneetseh.

Chapter 5

Hus in exile

The first important step taken by Hus after he had left Prague was to return temporarily to the city to appeal from the pope to Jesus Christ. He read this document himself from the pulpit in Prague. This appeal created a tremendous excitement, both among his friends and enemies. His enemies were filled with rage at what they called his blasphemy.

Royal commission to restore peace

At the same time, however, strenuous efforts were still kept up to bring about a compromise in the struggle which threatened to disrupt the whole country. On 3rd January 1413, a new synod was held, and there the question of how to restore peace to Bohemia was discussed. It was a foregone conclusion, however, that all these discussions were destined to come to naught. On the one hand, the king had no desire to carry out the pope's commands, and on the other hand, there was an irreconcilable difference between Hus's views of the Bible and the real Church of Christ, and the unyielding claim of supreme power over all men's consciences made by the Roman Catholic hierarchy. At last the king appointed a commission to go over the whole question.

The members of the commission began their work. They summoned the leading men of both parties, Hus's enemies Stanislav ze Znojma, Petr ze Znojma on the one side, and his friends Jan z Jesenice and Jakoubek ze Stříbra on the other. Hus could not appear, of course, as he had been practically exiled from Prague. Both sides promised to obey the decision of the commission. However, once more, irreconcilable differences stood in the way. King Václav became more and more impatient. Finally when Štěpán z Pálče and Petr ze Znojma refused to attend the meetings any further, on the ground that the proceedings were not impartial, the king lost control of his temper. In order to punish them for their obstinacy and disobedience, he banished them from his kingdom. Naturally enough, Hus was later accused of being the cause of their banishment, but as a matter fact, neither he nor Jerome was at Prague at the time.

The king's action was successful in one sense. Stanislav ze Znojma and Petr ze Znojma went to Moravia, and from this time onward they disappear from the story of Hus's life. Štěpán z Pálče went to the Bishop of Litomyšl, and he later accompanied the bishop to the Council of Constance. Štěpán achieved the baleful notoriety of being the protagonist in all the efforts, both open and underhanded, which were made to destroy Hus, his former friend and colleague.

Activities of Hus during his exile

Little detail is known of the life of Hus during the period of his exile. He first went to Kozí Hrádek,[73] a castle near the town of

---

[73] Pronounced Kozee Hradek. A castle (now ruined) where Hus spent time in exile in the autumn of 1412, and again from spring 1413 to spring 1414.

Ústí,[74] where afterward the famous settlement of Tábor was established, which became the real centre of Hussitism in Bohemia. This was undoubtedly due to Hus's presence there. Later, he went to the castle of Krakovec,[75] which was a little closer to Prague.

During all this time, Hus was busy in two ways: firstly in preaching, and secondly in writing. He had an extraordinary power of moving the people by sermons, which were at once clear and full of fervid devotion. This was now manifest by the immense crowds who flocked from all directions to hear him. It was during this time that he laid among the peasants the basis of that vast organization which afterwards became such a tremendous instrument in the hands of Žižka[76] and the two Hussite generals, Prokop Holý [Prokop the Great] and Prokop Malý[77] [Prokop the Lesser].

In the second place, he occupied the enforced leisure of his exile in composing those books in which he summed up the main points of his teachings. Perhaps no literary work of his was more important than his revision of an old translation of the Bible in the Bohemian language, made by an unknown writer of the fourteenth century. In this way, like Luther later, he not only made the Holy Scriptures accessible to the common people, but

---

[74] Pronounced Oostee. A town in Bohemia, adjacent to Tábor, about 50 miles (80 km) south of Prague. It should be distinguished from Ústí nad Labem, which is situated in the north of Bohemia, close to the present border with Germany.

[75] Pronounced Krakovets. A castle situated 36 miles (58 km) west of Prague. Hus spent his last months of exile in the castle, before going to the Council of Constance.

[76] Pronounced Zheeshka.

[77] Pronounced Prokop Holee and Prokop Malee.

also influenced strongly the development of his native tongue. Palacký says, 'As a writer in Bohemian he stood up for purity, and not only sought to regulate the language by means of firm rules, but he invented a new system of orthography [spelling] which recommended itself so much by means of its simplicity, precision, and consistency, that in the sixteenth century it was adopted by printers, and since then has been followed down to the present day.'

He especially devoted himself during this time to putting down in permanent form his reforming ideas. It was the spread of his writings, largely composed at this time, that made his influence grow more and more powerful throughout the land. This was especially true of his treatise on the Church.

The teaching of Hus

Before following him to Constance, then, it will be well to try to obtain as clear an idea as possible of his doctrines, especially insofar as they differed from those of the Church at that time. We shall thus be able better to understand the accusations made against him, and to appreciate the angry passions which made his trial a mockery and his condemnation a foregone conclusion.

It is not the place here to go into detail as to the whole creed of Hus. He was in harmony with the Church in many points which Protestantism has since abolished. Thus he believed devoutly in the Virgin Mary, in the worship of saints, and in the seven sac-raments. A great deal of discussion has taken place as to his atti-tude toward the doctrine of transubstantiation. This was one of the principal points urged against him at Constance. Yet when we carefully go over his writings, we cannot find any proof that he differed in this question from the established doctrine of the

Roman Catholic Church. While he followed Wycliffe in many respects, he did not follow him here. It is also a significant fact that he was not accused of this form of 'heresy' during the early years of his reforming activity. This was not raised as a complaint until 1412 when Michal de Causis, in his complaint to Pope John XXIII, declared that Hus had said from his pulpit in the Bethlehem Chapel that, after the consecration of the wafer on the altar, nothing but the natural bread remained. Hus, however, vigorously protested against this statement. Furthermore, in his third and last hearing before the Council of Constance, his accusers wished him to sign a recantation, he begged them not to force him to lie, in regard to a matter 'of which I know nothing, and concerning which witnesses have declared things which it never entered my head to say, especially that after consecration the bread still remained'.

The essential significance of Hus's teaching consists in his attitude toward two important doctrines, which he consistently taught from first to last—the ultimate authority of Holy Scripture, and the real constitution of the Church of Christ. His position on these two points makes him the true forerunner of Luther and Protestantism, and these teachings led to his condemnation and death. In these two doctrines he was diametrically opposed to the clergy and the Roman hierarchy. If he was right, then their power was based on false premises and it was threatened with ultimate destruction. All the patient building of the structure of ecclesiastical authority, with its marvellous system of hierarchical gradation from the lowest priest to the supreme pontiff, must crumble and fall to pieces. It was no mere academic thesis that was fought out at Constance; rather, it was the question of the very existence of the Roman Catholic Church.

The teaching of Hus about the Church

Although Hus did not dream of the logical conclusion of his teachings, yet they were in spirit the same as those held today by the true Protestant Churches.

It is not necessary to dwell on how vast a difference there was between Hus's view of the Church and that of the hierarchical system in the fifteenth century. In place of the simple organization of the apostolic community, a vast system had grown up, based on that of the secular Roman Empire. It was believed that God had deputed all his power on earth, both temporal and spiritual, to the pope as his own vicegerent. Not to believe in this was a mortal sin.[78] God was afar off, and could only be approached by man through the mediation of priests. The Church itself consisted in the whole body of the baptised. Whoever did not belong to the visible Roman Catholic Church was excluded from the mercy and grace of God, and outside the Roman Catholic Church, there was no salvation. On the other hand, those who conformed outwardly to the services, who attended the sacraments and humbly obeyed the ecclesiastical authorities, were considered to be members in good and regular standing of the 'Holy Church'. As everyone knows, all this was based on the words of Christ to Peter (Matthew 16:18–19): 'And I say also unto thee, that thou art Peter, and upon this rock I will build my church; and the gates of hell shall not prevail against it. And I will give unto thee the keys of the kingdom of heaven: and

---

[78] In Roman Catholicism, a 'mortal sin' is a gravely sinful act, which leads to damnation if a person does not repent of the sin before death. A mortal sin is defined as leading to a separation of that person from God's saving grace. In contrast, a 'venial sin' merely weakens a person's relationship with God.

whatsoever thou shalt bind on earth shall be bound in heaven: and whatsoever thou shalt loose on earth shall be loosed in heaven.'

Hus raised his voice against this whole ecclesiastical system. He declared that the Church consisted of the whole body of the elect, and that it is built alone on Christ, who is its sole head. In contrast to Hus, Štěpán z Pálče and Stanislav ze Znojma had declared in their debate with him that the pope as the successor of Peter was the head, and the cardinals as the successors of the apostles were the body of the Church—something that was held universally at that time.

Hus denied that Christ had meant that Peter was the head of the Church, and asserted that neither Peter nor any other apostle had claimed such authority. He further declared that the primitive Church was not a government of one man, but of all alike, as one can easily see from the Acts of the Apostles, and that the whole system of the papacy was false, based on the (alleged) Donation of Constantine. He showed how many popes had been heretics and men of corrupt life—in fact, one had been a woman in disguise. However, not only did he repudiate the papacy, but the whole system of the clergy, scourging them for their luxury, avarice, envy, and bitter quarrels.

By his criticism of these and many other features of Romanism, he practically destroyed the whole mediaeval Church. He wished to have it fundamentally reorganised. Every nation should have its own Church, independent of outside authority. The various members of it should be equal, laity as well as clergy. The temporal princes should defend the law of Christ and protect his servants. The clergy should attend strictly to their function of preaching and administering the sacraments, and should, by giving the example of a holy life, endeavour to draw all men to Christ. The laity should obey their natural lords in temporal affairs, and both rulers and people should be obedient to the clergy in spiritual things, yet not unconditionally even in this matter.

In all these things, we see that Hus was in harmony with Luther. Yet he was not a Protestant in the full sense of the word. He did not get beyond the Pelagian tenet of the mediaeval Church, that the human will is still capable of choosing good or evil without special divine aid. In all his utterances concerning grace, faith, and works he resembled Thomas Aquinas far more than he did the famous doctrine of Luther, 'The just shall live by faith.'

It is easy to conceive what bitterness such bold declarations concerning the Church must have produced among the members of the hierarchy. It was useless—indeed, it was foolhardiness—for him to go to the Council of Constance for, as it was a question of life and death for the papacy, there could be no possible compromise. There could not be the slightest doubt that Hus would be condemned unless he retracted. His friends tried to keep him from going. Indeed, he himself had a presentiment that he would never return. A calm consideration of the circumstances could have pointed to no other conclusion. To go to Constance meant going to inevitable death.

The teaching of Hus about Scripture

In his conception of the Church, Hus was in full agreement with the later movement of Protestantism. Still more is this true about his views concerning the Holy Scriptures. We have seen that when he was first appointed as preacher at the Bethlehem Chapel, he had been led to a profound study of the Bible, as a necessary means of preparation for his sermons. We have also seen that he spent part of his time during his exile in revising and preparing for the public a Bohemian translation of the Scriptures.

Yet in his public declarations concerning the Bible as the only ultimate authority in all questions of faith and conduct, Hus closely followed Wycliffe, especially the latter's treatise on *De Vertitate Sacrae Scripturae* [*Concerning the Truth of the Holy Scripture*]. He adopted the arguments he found there, and enlarged and carried them out to their logical conclusion. Every Christian is bound to believe all the truth, direct or indirect, which the Holy Ghost has laid down in the Bible. The claims of the doctors of the Church and the bulls of the pope are only to be attended to as far as they are based on the Scriptures. The same thing is true concerning the authority of the Synods, Councils, and the teachings of the Church Fathers. Hus did not deny these, except in such cases where they did not harmonise with the Bible. The Bible alone is the source of Christian truth. Repeatedly he emphasised this doctrine: it is the keynote in all his writings. And while it is true that it was his denunciation of the papacy and hierarchy which chiefly led his enemies to procure his death, it was the unshakable belief in the Holy Scriptures as the ultimate rule of faith that made him immovable in the face of hatred, abuse, and even death at the stake. He died a martyr's death because he would not give up his belief in the Bible.

The character of Hus

It was this firm and serene confidence in the power of truth that makes the name of Hus so glorious in the annals of the Church. As a thinker, he was not to be compared with Wycliffe. As a keen disputant and eloquent orator, he was inferior to his younger contemporary, Jerome of Prague, and he by no means had the administrative ability and indomitable energy that enabled Luther to carry out his mighty work.

His character was rather gentle than strong, and he was better fitted to be the spiritual director of his people than the leader of a bitter controversy marked by the noise of angry tongues. In a memorial sermon preached in Bethlehem Chapel after the death of Hus, an unknown preacher said, 'God gave him a practised tongue, so that he knew when he should speak. He had love and compassion for all men, even his enemies and persecutors. He was moral and blameless and devout, free from envy, avarice, and flattery.' But above all these attributes of a quiet and loving disposition, Hus possessed a deep love for truth and an unshakable faith in the power of God, which made him stand undismayed in the face of death, under the breastplate of a clear conscience.

Chapter 6

Journey to Constance

We have now come to the parting of the ways in the life of Jan Hus. The long period of contest, of vain efforts at compromise, had reached its climax.

The influence of Hus had spread over the whole extent of Bohemia, and his 'heretical' doctrines filled the members of the Roman Catholic Church with the bitterest hatred throughout all Christendom. A general feeling existed that something must be done to prevent the further spread of the mischief. There was only one way forward, and that was to submit the whole question to the decision of an Ecumenical Council.

Hus himself was far from realising the profound revolution and the irreconcilable differences with the papacy involved in his doctrines. He was eager to present his case before a General Council of the Church, instead of remaining confined to the authority of individuals such as the Archbishop of Prague and the Pope. It is difficult for us to see how he could hope for any favourable decision from such a Council, but it is beyond doubt that he desired to submit his case to it.

The agenda for the Council of Constance

The need of a General Council had been felt already for many years on other accounts. The discussion of Hus's doctrines had only lately become prominent, and it was more of an incidental motive rather than a fundamental one for calling such a Council. There were several other matters which imperatively demanded a settlement, chief among them being the healing of the great Western Schism, which had now become an intolerable scandal.

Of almost equal importance was the question of reforming the corruptions that existed in the Church. Morality among the clergy had reached its lowest ebb. The pictures drawn by Hus in his eloquent denunciations of their avarice, pride, and licentiousness were not a whit stronger than those painted by some of those who were later to become the chief instruments of his death. This was especially true of the great Gerson of the University of Paris and the French Cardinal d'Ailly. One of the avowed motives for calling the Council of Pisa in 1409 had been to purge the Church from immorality. However, immediately after the election of Alexander V, he had dissolved the Council without carrying out his pre-election promises. And so this deplorable state of immorality and greed continued until the Council of Constance was decided on.

All these things—and others of minor interest—were of long standing. In contrast, the 'heresy' of Bohemia was only taken into consideration a short time before convening the Council. Up to 1412, it had been largely a matter of local interest; after that, it became almost equal in importance with healing the schism and tackling the corruption of the Church.

97

The one man who was largely responsible for calling the Council was Zikmund Lucemburský (1368–1437), the brother of King Václav. Zikmund was the titular King of the Romans[79] and emperor-elect of the Holy Roman Empire. He was now fired with ambition to become emperor in the real sense of the word, and he desired to restore order and tranquillity throughout Europe. Religious questions were inseparably connected with political ones. Zikmund believed that he would gain prestige and influence through a successful Council—one which would result in healing the deep disorders in the Church. Such an outcome would be of inestimable value to his political ambitions.

The antipope John XXIII was then in Bologna, surrounded by many bitter enemies, threatened by Ladislaus, and rendered an object of contempt and disgust due to a life full of infamous vice. He had no liking or desire for a Council, which he foresaw only too well must end in disaster to himself. Nevertheless, Zikmund forced him to consent to it. As it had to take place, John XXIII would have preferred to stage it in some place under his own jurisdiction. However, he was also obliged to yield on this point, and to call the Council for Constance within the territory of the Holy Roman Empire.

The opening of the Council of Constance

The Council opened in November 1414, and was one of the most numerously attended the world had ever seen. The beautiful city of Constance is situated on the lake of the same name,

---

[79] 'King of the Romans' was the title used by the German king following his election by the princes. The title originated in the early 11th century. It was predominantly a claim to become Holy Roman Emperor and was dependent on coronation by the Pope.

and formed a fair background to the brilliant picture presented by the magnificently dressed princes of the Church and State, who crowded its narrow streets. It is said that as many as fifty thousand visitors attended, and that the numbers rose at times to one hundred thousand.

There were forty-five public and general sessions in all, from 16th November 1414 to 22nd April 1418. Beside the condemnation and death of Hus and Jerome, the other main outcomes included the deposition of antipope John XXIII, preparation for a real reformation of corruption by revealing the true condition of the clergy, and last (and most important of all, perhaps) the establishment of the doctrine that the authority of the Council is above that of the pope. In this brief biography of Hus, all these other matters must be passed over with mere mention.

The promise of safe-conduct

Hus himself had appealed to a General Council. He was now invited by Zikmund to attend the Council of Constance, under promise of a letter of safe-conduct. His friends warned him of the danger, as they knew the implacability of his enemies and the unreliability of the emperor. Although he did not allow himself to be dissuaded from his intention, yet the fears of his friends induced him to take certain precautions before starting. He returned to Prague in order to state his beliefs before the Provincial Council that had been called by the archbishop. On the day before it opened, he nailed to the church doors notices in Latin, German and Bohemian, stating that he was ready to appear before the assembly and give an account of his faith, and inviting all those who had any accusation to make against him to appear and bring forward their proofs.

He was not permitted to appear before the Provincial Council, however, but he did receive an important document from the papal inquisitor[80] in Bohemia, Nicholas of Nazareth. Nicholas declared that he had conversed with Hus a number of times, had often heard him preach, and had discussed several points of Holy Writ with him, but never had he found an error or heresy in him, but rather had found him in all his words and works to be a true and orthodox Christian. Hus likewise received the testimony of the Archbishop of Prague, Konrád z Vechty[81] [Conrad of Vechta], publicly given to certain noblemen, who sent it to the emperor in a letter, to the effect that he knew of no error or heresy in Hus.

Strong in his own conscience and fortified by these two testimonies as to his orthodoxy, Hus was now eager to go to Constance. On 1st September 1414, he wrote to Zikmund, declaring his willingness to appear before the Council. He requested a safe-conduct from the king, in order that he might proclaim his faith in public, adding the prophetic words: 'Nor, I hope, shall I be afraid to confess the Lord Christ, and, if necessary, to die for his most indubitable law.'[82]

Hus had already before this declared his willingness to die for his faith, in a letter he wrote to the rector of the University of Prague. It is worth quoting at length from this letter, as it shows

---

[80] An inquisitor was a Roman Catholic official with judicial or investigative functions. The Inquisitions were institutions designed to eliminate heresy and other things contrary to the doctrine or teachings of the Roman Catholic Church.

[81] Pronounced Konrat Sfechtee. He was Archbishop of Prague from 1413 to 1421.

[82] In the original Latin: *Nec spero verebar confiteri Christum dominum, et pro ejus lege verissima, si oportuerit, mortem pati.*

us the attitude of mind with which Hus looked forward to the contest between himself and his adversaries at Constance.

Venerable Rector, I have received a great consolation from your letter, in which you write among other things, 'The just shall not be cast down, whatever may happen to him.' I receive with gratitude this consolation. I cling to the words of Holy Writ, and say to myself that, if I am just, no evil whatsoever can so trouble me as to turn me away from the path of truth. If I live devoutly in Christ, I must suffer persecution in the name of Christ, for if it was necessary for him to suffer in order to enter into glory, we too must bear our cross and imitate him in his passion.

I declare then, venerable Rector, that I have never been crushed by persecution, that I am cast down only by my own sins and the errors of the Christian people. What are for me the riches of the world? What affliction can the loss of them cause to me? What care I for the loss of the favour of man? What is infamy to me, which when suffered in a humble spirit tries, purifies and glorifies the children of God, so that they shine and radiate like the sun in the kingdom of their Father? What care I for death? If they tear me away from this wretched life, I know that he who loses life here will triumph over death and find true life hereafter. But some men, blinded by luxury, vainglory [and] ambition, do not understand these things; others are turned away from the truth by fear, and linger on without patience or charity or virtue, in a strange perplexity. On one side, they are urged by the knowledge of the truth; on the other, by the fear of exposing their miserable body to death. As for me, I will expose my body to death (I hope with the aid of the Lord Jesus), if his mercy comes to my aid. For I do not desire to live in this corrupt world, unless I can lead to repentance both myself and others according to the will of God.

The accusations against Hus

In the meantime, his enemies were busy making preparation for their campaign of persecution. They had gathered all the accusations already made against him, and had formulated them, together with new material. All those who had ever heard Hus preach, or had any cause to bear witness against him, were invited to make a deposition under oath. To pay the necessary expenses, a collection was taken up among the clergy of Bohemia hostile to Hus. The amount thus gathered was forwarded to the Bishop of Litomyšl, Johann von Bucka[83] (John the Iron as he was called), who himself was about to start for Constance. The bishop was accompanied, among others, by Štěpán z Pálče, Hus's former friend, and now his most bitter enemy and unrelenting persecutor.

Written responses to the accusations

The accusations that had been drawn up against Hus were of two kinds: those extracted from his own writings, and those taken down by notaries from witnesses who declared they had heard him make certain heretical statements from the pulpit. Through a friend, while he was still in the castle at Krakovec, Hus received an abstract of the documents containing these witness accusations, and spent the remaining time before his departure in going over and answering them.

Most of these statements he declared to be false, such as that he had declared from the pulpit that after the Eucharist bread only remained (*i.e.*, that he denied the doctrine of transubstantiation), and that he had declared the efficacy of the sacrament to be

---

[83] Pronounced Yohann von Bootska.

neutralised when administered by a corrupt or wicked priest. He acknowledged, however, the truth of the statements made by certain witnesses, to the effect that he had declared that 'no one could be excommunicated, especially for money, except those whom God himself had excommunicated'. Nor did he deny having said that the Church could get along without a pope, and that he wished his soul might be where Wycliffe was.

To one man's declaration that he had denied the existence of the Church, Hus said no, but that he understood, as Augustine, Jerome, and others had done, the Church to be composed of all those who maintained that faith in Christ which had been taught by Peter and Paul at Rome.

To Michal de Causis, who declared that Hus had held all papal and episcopal indulgences to be worthless, and had declared that the pope was Antichrist and the Roman Catholic Church was a synonym for Satan, Hus answered that all these things thus stated were false. What he had said was that indulgences sold for money are not founded on the Scriptures; that the pope was Antichrist only when he sold the offices of the Church for money (*i.e.*, was guilty of simony), was proud, avaricious, and lived a life unworthy of a follower of Christ. A 'good pope' was not Antichrist.

Preparing to leave Bohemia

The time had now come for Hus to leave for Constance. On the day before his departure, 9th October 1414, he wrote a noble letter of farewell to his Bohemian friends, which deserves to be quoted here in its entirety:

I, Jan Hus, a priest and minister of Jesus Christ to all our beloved and faithful brothers and sisters, who have heard from
my mouth the divine word and have received the mercy and
peace of God and the Holy Spirit: may they continue to walk
without spot or blemish in the way of truth, through Jesus
Christ our Lord!

You know, dear brethren, that for a long time I have instructed
you in the faith, teaching you the Word of God, and not things
foreign to the truth. For I have always sought, seek still, and
shall seek even unto the end, only your salvation. I had resolved
before departing for Constance to refute all false accusations
and to confound those lying witnesses who wish to lead me to
destruction, but time has not allowed this, and I shall do it later.
You, then, who know these things, do not think, do not suppose that I shall meet unworthy treatment for any false doctrine. Abide in the truth, trusting in the mercy of God, who has
given you to know and defend the truth through me, his faithful preacher; and beware of false teachers.

As for me, armed with a safe-conduct from the emperor, I am
about to go forth to meet my numerous and mortal enemies.
These my enemies in the Council, more numerous than were
those of Christ, are among the bishops and doctors, and also
among the princes of this world and the Pharisees. But I trust
in Almighty God and in my Saviour, and I hope he will hear my
ardent prayers, that he will place prudence and wisdom in my
mouth, to the end that I may resist them; and that he will grant
me his Holy Spirit to fortify me in his truth, so that the gates of
hell may not turn me from it, and that I may confront with an
intrepid heart temptation, prison, and the sufferings of a cruel
death.

Christ suffered for his beloved; should we wonder then that he
has left us his example, in order that we endure patiently our-

selves all things for our own salvation? He is God and we are his creatures; he is the Lord and we are his servants; he is the master of the world and we are insignificant mortals; he has need of nothing, we are destitute of all; he has suffered, why should we not suffer likewise, especially when suffering is for us a purification?

Verily he cannot perish, who has confidence in Christ and who abides in his truth. Therefore, my beloved, pray to him earnestly to grant me his Spirit, that I may abide in his truth, and that he may deliver me from all evil. And if my death is to contribute to his glory, pray that it may come quickly, and that he may grant unto me to bear all my ills with constancy. But if it is better, in the interest of my salvation, that I return among you, we will ask of God that I may return from this Council without blemish; that is, that I may take away naught from the truth of the Gospel of Christ, in order that we may recognise more purely his light and leave unto our brethren a fair example to follow.

It may be you will never see my face again in Prague. But if the will of Almighty God should restore me to you, let us then move forward with a better heart in the knowledge and love of his law. The Lord is just and merciful, and he giveth peace to his own in this world and after death. May he watch over you, he who has purified us, his sheep, by the shedding of his own precious blood, which is the everlasting pledge of our salvation! May he grant unto you to accomplish his will, and when you shall have accomplished it, may he give you peace and eternal joy through Jesus Christ, together with all those who shall have remained in the truth![84]

---

[84] This letter was written in Bohemian, and a number of Latin versions have been made, That given by Palacký in his *Documenta* differs consid-

The day after he wrote this letter he started on his journey to Constance, in spite of the fact that the promised safe-conduct from the emperor had not come. This he did because he was anxious to be on hand when the Council should open. His state of mind was a mixed one. On the one hand, trusting in the protection of the emperor and his own good cause, he hoped to return in safety. On the other hand, it can be seen from the letter quoted above that he felt the seriousness of his situation. We can also see this from another letter, which he wrote before leaving Bohemia to a certain Master Martin. Hus requested him, however, not to open it until he was certain of his death. The letter ends with these words:

> Invoke the mercy of God for me, in order that he may deign to direct my life, and after the victory over the perverse powers of this world, over the flesh, the world and the devil, he may open unto me the celestial country in the last day. Farewell, then, in Jesus Christ, together with all those who obey his law. If you wish, you may keep my grey robe as a souvenir. Yet if you do not like the grey colour, dispose of it as seems best to you. Give also to my pupil, George, sixty pieces of silver or my grey robe, because he has served me well.

The journey to Constance

The parting from his friends was very painful. All were oppressed by a feeling that they should never see their beloved pastor again. In a letter written later in his prison at Constance he told how, on this occasion, a certain shoemaker, named Andrew Polonus, said to him: 'May God be with you! I can hardly hope that you will return safe and sound, my dear Master John,

---

erably from Bonnechose's French version, from which the above translation has been made.

you who cling so strongly to the truth. May the King, not of Hungary, but of Heaven, cover you with all his blessings, because of the true and excellent doctrines I have learned of you!'

He did not have to travel alone, however, for the two kings, Václav and Zikmund, gave him an escort consisting of three noblemen, who were to watch over his personal safety, both on his journey and during his sojourn in Constance. The most distinguished among them was Jan z Chlumu[85] [John of Chlum], and with him were Václav z Dubé[86] [Wenceslaus of Dubá] and Jindřich Lacembok z Chlumu[87] [Henry Latzenbock of Chlum]. The two former proved themselves to be men of courage and honour during the painful scenes that were soon to occur at Constance. Lacembok, however, publicly repudiated Hus's doctrines and approved his condemnation.

On 11th October, then, Hus set out in company with Václav z Dubé, Jan z Chlumu, and certain other Bohemians, among them Petr z Mladoňovic, to whom we owe the detailed story of Hus's life while in Constance. Lacembok met them later.

Hus was greatly pleased with his reception in the various towns and cities through which he passed. Everywhere he nailed up to the doors of the churches proclamations in Latin and German, stating that 'Master Jan Hus is now on his way to Constance, in order there to bear witness to the faith which he has hitherto confessed, confesses now, and ever shall confess, as God wills it, until his death. If any man has any error or heresy to accuse

---

85 Pronounced Yan Zchloomoo.
86 Pronounced Vatslaf Zdoobeh.
87 Pronounced Yeendrzheech Latsembock Zchloomoo.

him of, let him go to the Council, for there Master Jan Hus is ready to give satisfaction to every adversary.'

In a letter written from Nürnberg[88] in Germany we have a vivid picture of the scenes through which he passed on his journey. On approaching Pernau, he said:

> The priest was waiting for me with his curates. When I entered, he drank to my health in a large cup of wine. He and his friends listened to my teaching with a spirit of charity, and he said he had always been my friend. All the Germans saw me afterwards with pleasure in the new city. We went from there to Weiden, where we saw a great crowd, filled as it were with admiration, and when we had come to Salzbach, I said to the consuls and the elders of the city, 'I am that Jan Hus of whom you have doubtless heard much evil. Here I am. Satisfy yourself concerning the truth by asking me what questions you will.' After many questions, they received gladly all that I said to them.
>
> We came next to Nürnberg, where certain merchants who had preceded us had published my arrival. Wherefore the people remained in the public squares, looking and asking who Jan Hus was. Before dinner, the priest, John Heluvel, wrote me that he wished to have a long conversation with me. I invited him to come, and he came. Then the citizens and the Masters gathered together, desiring to see and to confer with me. Rising straightway from the table, I went to meet them, and as the Masters wished to confer with me, I said to them, 'I speak in

---

[88] A city in Bavaria, also known as Nuremberg in English. Hus spent time here on the way to the Council of Constance and his doctrines were well received. Later, Nürnberg was also the venue for Imperial Diets, which authorised the third and fifth (final) anti-Hussite crusades.

public, let those who wish to hear me listen,' and from this time until night we discussed in presence of the consuls and citizens. All the citizens and the Masters remained satisfied. 'Master,' they said, 'all that we have just heard is Catholic. We have taught these things many years; we have held them for true, and shall hold them so still. Surely you will return from this Council with honour.'

Cheered by all these evidences of goodwill toward him, and by the kind and noble friendship of Jan z Chlumu and Václav z Dubé, whom he called 'the heralds and advocates of truth', Hus went on his way to Constance, where he arrived on 3rd November 1414, after a journey of twenty days. John XXIII had arrived six days before. Emperor Zikmund was not to arrive before 25th December.

Chapter 7

Imprisonment, trial and martyrdom

With the arrival of Hus at Constance, the last act of the drama of his life began. He took lodgings in the house of a poor widow, situated on the public square near the palace of the pope. His arrival was the signal of renewed activity on the part of both friends and enemies.

Announcement of Hus's arrival in Constance

Jan z Chlumu and Jindřich Lacembok went the next day to the pope to announce the arrival of their protégé, declaring that he was furnished with a safe-conduct from Emperor Zikmund, and requesting the pope to see that this safe-conduct should not be violated. In the words of the German historian, Hermann von der Hardt, the messengers of Hus were received courteously, and are said to have brought back the answer from the pope: 'Even if Jan Hus had slain his own brother, he would not allow him to be injured in any way, as far as he was able to prevent it, as long as he remained in Constance.'

Controversy about the letter of safe-conduct

Thus matters seemed to begin auspiciously for the Bohemian reformer. This assurance of friendliness on the part of the pope

110

was supplemented the next day by the arrival of Václav z Dubé, who brought the famous safe-conduct promised by the Emperor Zikmund to Hus—as we have seen, Hus had come to Constance before he had received it.

A bitter controversy has arisen over the whole subject of this safe-conduct, which, as we shall see later, did not save its holder. On the one hand, the friends of Hus looked on Zikmund's betrayal of his own written word as a contemptible act of weakness and treachery. On the other hand, the defenders of the Church declared that the emperor could not do otherwise. Eberhard Dacher, an eyewitness of the Council, sums up this side of the argument in these words: 'Zikmund was persuaded, after a great many words, that by virtue of the decretals,[89] he was dispensed from keeping his faith with a man accused of heresy.' It was further said that the emperor had no authority to grant the safe-conduct without the consent of the Council, especially in matters of faith, and that the emperor acquiesced in this decision, like a good son of the Church.

The Council itself later passed two decrees, in order to justify the action of the emperor before the world. How successful they were in this may be gathered from an anecdote told of Charles V over a hundred years later. When urged to violate his safe-conduct to Luther at the Diet of Worms,[90] Charles replied, 'I do not wish to blush as Zikmund did,' alluding to the tradition that in Hus's last appearance before the Council he declared that he had come of his own accord to the Council, under the public

---

[89] Papal decrees concerning points of canon law.
[90] An Imperial Diet was a general assembly of the Imperial Estates of the Holy Roman Empire. Diets occurred at irregular intervals. The Diet of Worms was conducted from 28th January to 26th May 1521.

faith of the emperor present there. It is said that, when Hus pronounced these words 'he looked earnestly at Zikmund, who could not help blushing.' It is certain that posterity will always agree with Jacques Lenfant that 'Jan Hus was a victim not only to the passion of his enemies, but also to the weakness and superstition, not to say the treachery, of the emperor.'

Arrest of Hus

For several days Hus lived quietly and unmolested in his lodgings. He was free enough in many respects, but was forbidden to attend the public mass because of his ecclesiastical status, namely, his having been excommunicated. In the meantime, his enemies were actively at work poisoning the minds of all against him. De Causis and Páleč were especially active, causing placards to be put up everywhere, denouncing Hus as an excommunicated heretic, and distributing garbled extracts from his books to the pope and the cardinals. When Hus complained of this to the pope, the latter said, 'What can I do? They who have done it are your own countrymen.'

The machinations of his enemies soon bore fruit. Although Hus abstained from being present at public mass, he performed the mass privately in his own lodgings and a large number of people came to it. When ordered by the Bishop of Constance[91] to desist, it is said that he refused to do so in no gentle terms. Whether this is true or not, De Causis and Páleč finally prevailed upon the cardinals to arrest him. This was not done openly, but in an underhand way. A deputation was sent to Hus to summon him to appear before the cardinals, there to give an account of his

---

[91] Otto III von Hachberg (1388–1451) was Bishop of Constance from 1410 to 1434.

doctrines. They had taken the precaution to station a number of armed soldiers in the neighbourhood to prevent any disturbance. Hus replied to this summons that he had not come to Constance to speak to the cardinals, but to appear before the entire Council, and to answer all questions that might be asked. Yet nevertheless he declared himself ready to go to the cardinals, and if he were there questioned concerning his faith, he would rather prefer to die than to deny the truth he had learned from the gospel.

Hus left his lodgings, accompanied by Jan z Chlumu. When he was introduced into the presence of the cardinals, they said to him, 'Master John, it is said that you have taught and disseminated many errors in Bohemia, and therefore we have sent for you, wishing to inquire of you if this is true.'

Hus answered, 'Most reverend fathers, be it known unto you that, rather than to hold error, I should prefer to die. Behold, I have freely come to the sacred Council, ready, if I have erred, to be corrected.'

Then the cardinals said, 'Verily these are good words,' and they went away, each one to his own affairs, leaving Hus under the guard of the armed men.

A short time afterward a monk was sent to him as a spy, under the pretence of a friendly conversation. The monk pretended to be a simple, unlearned man, desirous of being instructed in certain questions, especially that of transubstantiation. His object was evidently to get Hus to confess his belief that only bread remained on the altar after the mass. As we have already seen, this was not Hus's position. He bluntly declared so to the priest, whom he began to suspect of not being as ignorant as he pretended to be. When this false monk asked him his opinion as to the human and divine nature of Christ, Hus turned to Jan z Chlumu and said in Bohemian, 'Verily this monk says he is a simple and ignorant man, yet he is not so simple, since he asks questions concerning the deepest subjects.' Turning to the monk he said, 'Brother, you say you are simple, but I think you are double [duplicitous].' It was afterwards found out that the monk was one of the most eminent Roman Catholic theologians of Italy.

Imprisonment of Hus

In the meantime, Páleč and Michal de Causis and other enemies of Hus, had persuaded the cardinals by continual urging, that they ought not to let Hus go free again. And so, when evening had come, they sent word to Jan z Chlumu that he could leave when he pleased, but as for Hus, he should remain in the pope's palace.

Filled with indignation, Jan z Chlumu went to the pope and complained bitterly of this action, which not only violated the safe-conduct that Hus had received from the emperor, but likewise was contrary to the oral promise of the pope himself, made a short time before, that he would protect him. All of this was to no avail, however, for the pope weakly and hypocritically laid the blame on the cardinals and the bishops.

About ten o'clock that night Hus was removed from the papal palace to the house of the cantor of the cathedral of Constance, where he was kept under guard for eight days. Then he was taken to a Dominican monastery situated on an island in the Rhine. Here he was thrown into a dark dungeon, in the immediate neighbourhood of a sewer, where he remained until 24th March

1415. As may be easily understood, his health suffered in this wretched hole. He developed a serious fever so that his life was despaired of, and Pope John XXIII sent his own physician to attend him.

While all this was going on Hus's enemies went about their nefarious schemes. Michal de Causis prepared a document containing eight articles, which he presented to the pope. These articles contained the gist of the accusations against Hus, and are here given in outline:

> It is declared that Hus had publicly taught that the sacrament ought to be administered in two kinds, and that he had taught publicly both in the university and in church, or that at least he holds the opinion, that in the sacrament of the altar the bread remains bread after the consecration.

> He is accused of saying that ministers in a state of mortal sin cannot administer the sacrament, and that on the contrary any person may do it, provided he is in a state of grace. He has taught that by the Church ought not to be understood the pope, cardinals, archbishops, and clergy, and that this is a wicked definition invented by the Schoolmen; further, that the Church ought not to possess temporalities,[92] and that the secular lords may take them away from the Churches and ecclesiastics with impunity; that Constantine and the other princes were guilty of an error in endowing the Church; that all priests are of equal authority, and that consequently the ordinations reserved to the pope and bishops are the mere effect of their ambition; that the Church has no longer the power of the keys when the pope, cardinals, bishops, and all, the clergy are in a state of mortal sin, which may be the case; finally he, Hus, despises ex-

---

[92] Secular possessions of the Church.

communication, having all along celebrated the divine office[93] during his journey.

After two more articles, along the same line as the preceding, he discussed the conduct of Hus. De Causis accused him among other things of having been the prime cause of the German students and professors seceding from the University of Prague in 1409, and of having defended the doctrines of Wycliffe against the will of the University, which had condemned them, and of gathering around him heretics and enemies of the Church. From these things, he inferred that if Jan Hus were not severely treated by the Council, he would do the Church more harm than ever any heretic did since the reign of Constantine, and prayed that the pope would immediately appoint commissioners to examine him, and doctors to read carefully his works.

Attempts to free Hus

In the meantime, Jan z Chlumu left nothing undone to secure the release of Hus. He wrote to the emperor, who had not yet come to Constance, complaining of the way in which his safe-conduct had been treated, and the emperor, who had not yet been persuaded by casuistical remarks to break his word, fell into a rage and ordered that Hus be released. This order was not obeyed, and Jan z Chlumu in his indignation nailed up to the doors of the churches throughout the city the following manifesto:

---

[93] This is known by various names in the Roman Catholic Church, such as the Breviary or the Liturgy of Hours. It consists of the official set of prayers 'marking the hours of each day and sanctifying the day with prayer'.

I, Jan z Chlumu, make known to all who shall see or hear these presents [this document], that Master Jan Hus, Bachelor of Divinity, having come to Constance there to give an account of his faith in a public hearing, under the safe-conduct and protection of the most serene prince, Lord Zikmund, King of the Romans and of Hungary, for which he has the king's letters patent. Yet notwithstanding this safe-conduct, Master Jan Hus has been apprehended and is actually detained in a prison of this city. And though the pope and cardinals have been very seriously required by solemn ambassadors from the king to recommit him to my care, they have hitherto refused and still do refuse to do it, to the great contempt of the safe-conduct of the king. Therefore I, Jan z Chlumu, do declare in the king's name that the imprisonment and detaining of Master Jan Hus is not at all pleasing to the King of the Romans, and that they have taken advantage of his absence to commit an act, which they never would have dared to do if he had been present. When he arrives, every one shall know how he resents this contemptuous treatment of his safe-conduct. Dated at Constance on Christmas Eve, 1414.

Continued imprisonment

With the arrival of Emperor Zikmund the next morning, however, all these hopes gradually began to die out. Endowed with many and brilliant qualities, filled with ambition to restore once more the glory of the Holy Roman Empire, Zikmund had brought about the calling of the Council, not so much for the good of the Church as for his own ambitions. He well knew that if he succeeded in reforming the corruption of the Church and in putting an end to the Western Schism, his own glory and prestige would be prodigiously enhanced. When he saw that by persisting in protecting Hus he was in danger of dissolving the Council, he basely deserted him and left him in prison.

In Bohemia the news of Hus's imprisonment filled the nobles with rage, but the indignant letters they wrote to the emperor only resulted in having their countryman more closely confined.

The story of the next few months in Hus's life is a monotonous one. To repeat the details given by Von der Hardt, Lenfant, and Petr z Mladoňovic would be out of place in this brief sketch. We can only cast a glance at the epoch-making events that occurred outside his prison, and then look for a moment at Hus himself and his life before the final catastrophe came.

The Council of Constance and the papacy

The Council met from time to time, and discussed the important items of business that had called them together.

Sermons were preached on the corruption of the clergy and the tyranny of the pope, equalling, if not surpassing, in freedom of utterance, anything ever said by Wycliffe and Hus.

The whole year of 1415 was full of stirring events, and was not to close before the death of Hus. Almost as soon as Emperor Zikmund arrived, a coolness sprang up between him and the pope. The pope, who saw he could expect nothing good from the Council, now only sought a means of escape, and although a strict watch was kept on the gates, he succeeded in accomplishing his plan, through the help of the Duke Friedrich IV [Frederick IV] of Austria. For a moment, it looked as if the Council would have to be dissolved, but the emperor declared that it was still in session. This did more than anything else to strengthen the claim of Gerson and the University of Paris that the authority of the Council was superior to the pope, a doctrine that has distinguished the French Roman Catholic Church ever since. A

118

few months after, on 29th March 1415, the antipope John XXIII was deposed from the papacy.

Arrival of Jerome

Another important event was the arrival in Constance of Jerome of Prague, the faithful friend and disciple of Hus. When Hus was about to leave for the Council, Jerome is said to have exhorted him to be faithful in holding on to what he had so often preached, and declared that if he should hear that Hus were ill-treated at Constance he would follow him there. Carrying out his promise he arrived there on 24th April, but for some unknown reason he left the same day. Jerome went to Überlingen and wrote a letter to the pope from there, asking for a safe-conduct, and then he started for Bohemia again. He was arrested, however, and brought back in chains to Constance and cast into prison.

Worsening prison conditions for Hus

In the meantime, Hus remained a prisoner. He had been removed from the Dominican monastery to that of the Franciscans. At the time of the antipope's flight, Hus's friends hoped to persuade Emperor Zikmund to release him. This was in vain, for the emperor now yielded to the unremitting demands of Hus's enemies. He turned Hus over to the care of the Bishop of Constance, and ordered that the trial against him should be carried on with the utmost severity.

Now Hus was treated with still greater cruelty, and was carried in chains in a boat to Schloss Gottlieben [Gottlieben Castle], a short distance down the River Rhine from the Constance. He was kept there in a high tower, with his feet bound by chains, and at night his hands were chained to the wall. He was fed on wretched food and was scarcely able to move because of his fetters, and remained at Gottlieben from 24th March to the beginning of June.

We catch a glimpse of the inner life of Hus during all these weary months when we read his letters to his friends, written while in prison. We see his patience and his gratitude for all the kindness shown him by the prison keepers. We also see how he lost all bitterness against his persecutors, praying God to forgive even his arch-enemy, Páleč. We see his thoughtfulness in the midst of his own tribulations for the welfare of his friends. Moreover, we see his hopes and fears for himself and his confidence in God that justice would prevail, not only in his own case, but also in the whole reforming movement that he had done so much to spread.

In a letter written on 24th June to his Bohemian friends, he uttered what some have looked upon as a prophecy of Luther and his Reformation:

> Would that I might manifest the iniquity I have learned to know, in order that the faithful servants of God may be on their guard against it. But I hope that God will send after me champions stronger than I, who will better lay bare the sin of Antichrist, and who will expose themselves to death for the truth of the Lord Jesus Christ, who will give to you and to me eternal glory.

In addition, in another letter, speaking about a dream he had, in which he saw the pictures in Bethlehem Chapel destroyed by his enemies, after which many painters had made new ones, he says:

I hope that the life of Christ, that I painted through his Word at Bethlehem in the hearts of men, and that his enemies have tried to destroy by forbidding all preaching in the chapel and wishing to raze it to the ground; I hope, I say, that this same life will be better drawn in the future by preachers more eloquent than I, to the great joy of the people who cling with all their heart to Christ. I shall rejoice myself when I shall awake—that is, when I shall rise again from the dead.

We must now leave all other things and turn our attention to the closing scenes of that drama, the details of which are so touching, and which was to end in the death of Hus. In spite of the fact that he had to come to Constance in order to defend his doctrine before the Council, months had passed by without bringing an opportunity for him to appear before his accusers publicly. John XXIII had appointed a commission to examine the charges against him, and after the flight of this antipope, a new commission had been appointed by the Council. Many visits had been made by members of this commission and others to Hus in prison. They had argued with him repeatedly, and although he constantly reiterated his desire to defend his case before the Council in public, he did not now refuse to discuss the various accusations made against him. All efforts to make him confess that he had been in error were unavailing, however. He constantly declared that he would only recant if they would show him to be in error based on the Holy Scriptures.

Final efforts to release Hus from prison

We have seen that the attempt made to obtain Hus's liberty at the time of the pope's flight only resulted in a harsher imprisonment. A final effort was made by his friends in Constance on

13th May. A memorial[94] was written and read by Petr z Mladoňovic to the Council, protesting against the imprisonment of the Reformer and the slanders of his enemies. Petr also demanded that Hus should be set free, in order that he might regain health and strength, so that he might be in a fit condition to answer his enemies. Furthermore, the lords of Bohemia offered themselves as securities that Hus should not run away before his case was settled.

First public hearing for Hus

Although they did not succeed in securing Hus's release from prison, they did succeed in extorting a promise from the Council and emperor to give him a public hearing. The date was set for 5th June. This in itself was joyful news to Hus. The private hearings, which had been many, had turned out to be entirely unsatisfactory, and were often accompanied by insult and violence. In one of his letters he tells how Michal de Causis was there holding a paper in his hand and stirring up the Latin Patriarch of Constantinople[95] to force him to answer his questions. 'God has permitted Páleč and him,' he cries out, 'to rise up against me for my sins. Michal examines all my letters and writings, and Páleč reports all the conversations we have had together during many years.'

It was with a revival of courage and hope that Hus now learned that he was to be heard before the Council. He was in poor

---

[94] A statement of facts as the basis of a petition.
[95] Jean de la Rochetaillée (died 1437) was titular Patriarch of Constantinople from 1412 to 1423. It should be noted that the Latin Patriarchate was founded after the Crusades, and should not be confused with the Eastern Orthodox Patriarchate of Constantinople, an office that existed before and after the Roman Catholic one.

condition to undergo such a trial, being worn out by long imprisonment, suffering many painful diseases—toothache, haemorrhages, gravel, and pains in the head. He was brought back to Constance, as his prison in Gottlieben was now occupied by John XXIII, who had been caught and was returned to Constance.

Constance Minster, venue of the Council of Constance

On 5th June, a great crowd gathered together in the refectory of the Franciscan monastery, where the Council was to sit. It seemed at first as if they were going to condemn him without being heard, but Petr z Mladoňovic hastily departed and apprised Jan z Chlumu and Václav z Dubé of his suspicions, and they informed the emperor immediately. The latter then sent the

Elector Palatine[96] and the Burgrave of Nürnberg[97] to the Council, forbidding them in his name to try Hus without a fair hearing.

The scene that followed was a disgraceful one. It was at once evident that Hus could not obtain a fair hearing before these men, who were animated by the bitterest hatred toward him. Lenfant in his *History of the Council of Constance* says:

> As soon as he came in, they put his works into his hands, which he owned and offered to retract if any error was found in them. After this, they began with the reading of the articles. But they had scarce made an end of the first, with the evidence supporting it, when so terrible a noise arose that the Fathers could not hear one another, much less the answers of Jan Hus. When the clamour had subdued a little, Hus, offering to defend himself by the authority of the Scriptures and the Fathers, was interrupted as if he had spoken nothing to the purpose, and they set upon him with reproach and banter. If he chose to hold his peace, his silence was looked upon as approbation, though he declared he was forced to be silent because they would not hear him. In short, everything passed with so much confusion that, for the Council's honour, the most judicious of the members advised the putting off of the affair to another day.

---

[96] From the 13th century onwards, seven Prince-Electors had the privilege of electing the King of the Romans, who would be crowned by the Pope as Holy Roman Emperor. The three ecclesiastical Electors were the Archbishops of Mainz, Trier and Cologne, and the four secular Electors were the King of Bohemia, the Count Palatine of the Rhine, the Duke of Saxony and the Margrave of Brandenburg.

[97] A title for the ruler of a castle, especially a royal or episcopal castle, as well as a castle district or fortified settlement or city. The burgrave held the noble rank of a count, and had judicial powers.

Second public hearing for Hus

The second hearing took place two days afterward, on 7th June. A certain solemnity was added to it by an almost total eclipse of the sun that had occurred earlier in the day. The presence of the emperor meant that this meeting passed more quietly than the previous one.

Two classes of accusations had been made against Hus—those based on the report of witnesses as to what he had said and done, and which had been written up by De Causis, and those based on extracts from Hus's own writings, probably drawn up by Páleč. Out of these, he was accused of having taught thirty-nine different heretical doctrines, most of them being drawn from his book on the Church.

The whole of this session was devoted to the first class of accusations. As we have seen before, Hus had denied already some of these and confessed to others. The old accusations were repeated, that he had denied the doctrine of transubstantiation, had spread Wycliffe's doctrines throughout Bohemia, had caused the emigration of the German members of the University, and had disobeyed the Church and caused a great schism among the people of Bohemia, and especially of Prague.

Before he was taken from the Council, Pierre d'Ailly, the Cardinal of Cambrai,[98] reproached him in the emperor's presence with having said that, if he had not wanted to come to the Council, neither the king nor the emperor could have made him, at which a great murmuring was heard in the assembly.

---

[98] Cambrai is an archdiocese of the Roman Catholic Church in the north of France, near the present-day border with Belgium.

At this, Jan z Chlumu boldly exclaimed: 'Jan Hus has asserted nothing but what is true, for though I am one of the meanest lords in Bohemia, I would undertake to defend him for a year against all the forces of the king and emperor. Much more could the other nobles do, who are more powerful than I.'

Then the emperor said to Hus:

> We advise you to maintain nothing obstinately, and to submit yourself with all obedience to the authority of the Council in all the articles which have been exhibited and solidly proved against you, which if you do we will take care that for the sake of the king and kingdom of Bohemia you shall retire with the goodwill of the Council, after you have made tolerable penance and satisfaction; but if not, the Council will know how to deal with you. For our part, we shall be so far from supporting you in your errors and obstinacy, that we will with our own hands kindle the fire to burn you, rather than tolerate you further. You will do well, then, to stand to [stand ready for] the judgment of the Council.

Third public hearing for Hus

The next day, the third and last hearing of Hus took place. The thirty-nine articles purporting to be drawn from his writings were read and discussed.

Here, as in the previous hearing, he acknowledged some of the articles as his, but denied those which had been garbled by his enemies, especially by Štěpán z Pálče. When the tenth article was read, in which it was said that the vicar of Christ was only so in truth if he imitated the life of Christ, and the words of Hus's answer were read, 'If the pope lives after another manner than St Peter did, if he is covetous, he is the vicar of Judas Iscariot

126

who courted the wages of iniquity, by selling Jesus Christ.' While this answer was being read, the fathers of the Council stared at one another and shook their heads with a sneer. Again, when a passage was read in which Hus spoke of those who deliver a heretic to the secular arm before conviction, comparing them to the high priests and Pharisees, a great murmur arose among the cardinals and bishops, and when he attempted to explain his appeal to Christ, they all burst out laughing at him.

A dramatic incident occurred concerning the statement that, if a pope or bishop or prelate is in deadly sin, he is neither pope nor bishop nor prelate. Hus had acknowledged this, and had quoted in support of his statement the words of Jerome, Augustine, Gregory, and others, adding, 'And even a king in deadly sin is not worthily a king before God, according to those words which God said to Saul by the Prophet Samuel, "Because thou hast rejected my word, I will reject thee from being a king."'

While this article and Hus's answer to it were being read, the emperor was talking at a window with the Elector Palatine and the Burgrave of Nürnberg. During this conversation, they said amongst other things that they never had seen a more pernicious heretic than Jan Hus. Cardinal Cambrai called the emperor's attention to what Hus had said, and Hus was commanded to repeat the words that had just been read, *i.e.*, that a king in deadly sin is unworthy of God. The only answer the emperor made was, 'There is no man living without a fault.' However, Cardinal Cambrai cried out angrily, 'Was it not enough for you to have abased the clergy, but you must do the same with the king?'

Attempts to make Hus recant

At the end of the session, strenuous efforts were made to induce Hus to retract. Cardinal Cambrai addressed him as follows:

> You see how many heinous crimes you have been accused of. You are now to consider well what you are to do. The Council has but two things to propose to you, of which you will do well to embrace the first, which is to submit yourself humbly to their sentence and decree, and to undergo, without repining, whatever they shall please to inflict upon you; in which case you will be treated with all the gentleness and humanity possible. If on the contrary you choose the other way, which is to defend any of those articles laid to your charge, and to demand another hearing for that purpose, you shall not indeed be refused a hearing. But consider well that here are a great many persons of weight and knowledge, who have produced such strong arguments against your articles that I much fear while you persist in your defence, your obstinacy will expose you to some fatal consequence. This I say not as your judge, but as your monitor.

Other prelates added their exhortations and entreaties, to all of which Hus replied with a lowly countenance:

> Reverend Fathers, I have already said more than once that I came here of my own free will, not to maintain anything with obstinacy, but to receive instruction, if it should appear that I have been mistaken. I entreat you then that I may be allowed to explain my sentiments more at large, and if I do not support them by certain and solid arguments, then I will readily conform to your instructions, as you desire.

Immediately after that, the sentence of the Council was read to him:

1. That he should confess to have erred in holding those articles which had been alleged against him, and ask pardon.
2. That he should promise upon oath never to hold or teach them anymore.
3. That he should retract them in public.

This Hus firmly declined to do, 'for to abjure is to renounce an error that hath been held. But as there are many errors laid to my charge which have never entered my head, how can I renounce them by oath?'

He refused to accept the casuistical ways of escape from this dilemma suggested by the emperor, or to accept the suggestion made by the Cardinal of Florence of an abjuration 'as gentle and equitable as he perhaps would accept'.

The emperor was now at the end of his patience and spoke to him as follows:

> You are of age, and after what I have now repeated to you, it is at your option to choose the alternative. We cannot but give credit to the witnesses against you. Therefore if you are wise, you will submit with a contrite heart to the penance that shall be imposed upon you by the Council. You will renounce your errors because they are manifest, and you will swear to teach and hold them no longer, but on the contrary to oppose them as long as you live; otherwise there are laws according to which the Council will judge you.

Judgment against Hus

Hus was now taken back to prison, tired out in body and mind, but of an unbroken spirit. When he had gone, the emperor addressed the Council and said, 'You have heard the articles laid to the charge of Jan Hus. In my opinion, there is not one among them that does not deserve punishment by fire. If therefore he does not retract them all, I am for having him burnt.'

Thus ended the last hearing of Hus before the Council. He had had an opportunity of facing his accusers while the long list of accusations was made against him. However, in spite of this, the whole proceeding was nothing but a mockery of justice. From the first, it was a foregone conclusion that one of two things must happen: he must either recant or be condemned. The differences between him and his adversaries were irreconcilable, and no amount of argument could change the fact. On both sides there was an unshaken determination not to yield. In Hus's case it amounted to a heroic courage rarely seen even in the annals of martyrdom. Alone, sick and suffering, weakened by months of close confinement, he never for a moment hesitated or lost his firmness. Quiet, gentle, yet firm as a rock, he withstood all insults, ridicule and threats.

Further attempts to make Hus recant

The same firmness was shown after the Council, when numerous efforts were made to make him recant. Even his bitterest and most unrelenting enemy, Páleč, visited him in prison and urged him to yield, telling him he ought not to fear the shame of a recantation, but only to think of the good which would follow. To this Hus answered, 'The disgrace of being condemned and burned is greater than that of recanting sincerely. What shame, then, should I fear in recanting? But tell me, Páleč, what would you do if you were sure that errors were imputed to you wrongly? Would you retract them? That is hard,' he said, and burst into tears.

The motives that led Hus to hold out against all these entreaties were not those of pride of opinion, or of mere obstinacy. This is clearly shown in one of his noblest letters written to his friends.

These are the things that the Council has often demanded of me. But they imply that I renounce and recant, that I accept a penitence, and this I cannot do without going against the truth in many things. For I would perjure myself by confessing errors which are falsely attributed to me. Furthermore, I should give an occasion of great scandal to the people of God who have listened to my preaching, and it would be better that a millstone were hanged about my neck and that I should be plunged to the bottom of the sea. Finally, if I should act thus to escape a momentary confusion and brief suffering, I should fall into disgrace and suffering far more terrible, unless I repented before my death. This is why I have thought, in order to strengthen myself, on the seven martyred Maccabees,[99] who preferred to be cut to pieces rather than eat meat prohibited by God. I thought also of the holy Eleazar, who according as it is written did not even wish to confess that he had eaten forbidden food, for fear of leaving a bad example to posterity, but preferred a martyr's death.[100] Having, then, before my eyes many saints of the new dispensation who have accepted martyrdom, rather than to consent to sin, how shall I who have exhorted others in my sermons to patience and firmness fall into perjury and vile deceits, and offend by my example many children of our Lord? Far be it from me! Far be it from me! Our Lord and Saviour Jesus Christ will reward me plentifully, and will give me in my trials the help of patience.

Owing to the desire of the emperor and others to secure his recantation, the formal condemnation was put off for several

---

[99] An account in the apocryphal books of 2 and 4 Maccabees.
[100] An account in 2 Maccabees, chapter 6.

weeks. On 15th June, the Council declared heretical the doctrine of Jakoubek ze Stříbra concerning the use of the Eucharist in two kinds, which had grown important in Bohemia after Hus's departure, and which he had approved in his letters from prison. On 24th June, they resolved to burn Hus's books, hoping in this way to bend his stubborn will. However, all was in vain, as may be seen from his letter to his friends in Bohemia, exhorting them not to cease reading his writings, nor to give them up to be burnt.

The day before his sentence and death the emperor made one final attempt to persuade him to recant. He sent a distinguished delegation, consisting of four bishops, accompanied by Hus's faithful friends, Václav z Dubé and Jan z Chlumu, to ask him 'whether he would abjure those articles which he acknowledged as his, and as to those which he did not own, though they were proved, whether he would swear that he did not hold them, and that he had no other sentiments than those of the Church'.

Hus replied that he stood by the declaration he had made on 1st July. This was a declaration he had given to another deputation that had visited him on that day, and reads as follows:

> Fearing to offend God and to perjure myself, I am not willing to abjure any of the articles that have been exhibited against me by false evidences, and which I call God to witness, were never preached nor defended by me, as they are laid to my charge. As to the articles extracted from my books, I declare that if there is any one of them that carries any errors in it I abhor it, but am not willing to abjure one of them, for fear of offending the truth and the sentiments of the holy doctors. And if it were possible that my voice reach the uttermost parts of the earth as clearly as every lie, and as all my sins shall be made manifest at

the last day, I would heartily revoke before the whole world every falsehood or error which I may have said or conceived. This is what I declare, and what I freely and voluntarily write.

It was this written declaration to which, as his ultimatum, Hus now referred the last commission who visited him.

On this occasion a noble and touching incident occurred, related as follows by Petr z Mladoňovic:

> When they were taking Hus out of prison to meet the commissioners, Jan z Chlumu spoke to him: 'Master John, I am a layman, and cannot presume to offer you advice. Therefore, if you feel yourself guilty of any one of those things of which you are accused, do not be ashamed to be instructed by them and to recant. But if you do not feel you are guilty, follow your own conscience, and do not be guilty of falsehood in the sight of God, but rather stand fast in the truth which you have known, even unto death.'

> And Hus, shedding tears, answered humbly: 'Sir John, know this. If I felt that I had written or preached any errors against the law and Holy Mother Church, I would humbly recant, as God is my witness.'

Formal condemnation and degradation

We now come to the last sad scene in the drama of Hus's life. The fifteenth session of the Council was held on 6th July 1415. The chief business of that session was the condemnation and sentencing of Hus. Everyone of note in the city was present, either out of curiosity or to rejoice in the final destruction of a famous and obstinate 'heretic'. The emperor, with all the princes of the empire, was also present, lending solemnity to the occasion.

A platform in the form of a table of a certain height was erected in the middle of the church, upon which were the priestly garments in which Hus was to be clothed before the ceremony of his degradation began. He himself was placed on a high stool before the table, in order that all the people might see him. He made a prayer in a loud voice, while at the same time Bishop Arrigoni of Lodi (in northern Italy) began his sermon.

The text of the sermon was from Paul, 'That the body of sin might be destroyed', and in it the preacher showed among other things how much heresies distract and harm the Church. After the sermon the proceedings against Hus were begun, but not before a decree of the Council was read, forbidding all manifestations of either approval or disapproval, on pain of excommunication and imprisonment, not excepting kings and princes. The first thing read was the condemnation of additional articles by Wycliffe, for we must bear in mind that Hus's errors were considered to be fundamentally based on those of Wycliffe. After the reading of these articles, some thirty more of Hus's were read. When all these preliminaries were over, the Bishop of Concordia read two sentences, one condemning the books of Hus to be burnt, the other condemning Hus himself to be degraded from his office as priest.

It is worthwhile recording this latter sentence in the actual words in which it was read:

> The sacred Council of Constance, after having called upon the name of Jesus Christ, and having the fear of God before their eyes, does pronounce, decree, and declare that the said Jan Hus was and is a real and notorious heretic, who has publicly taught and preached errors and heresies long ago condemned by the Church of God; that he has advanced several things scandal-

ous, offensive to pious ears, rash and seditious, to the great reproach of the divine majesty, to the offence of the whole Church, and to the detriment of the Catholic faith; that he has trampled the keys of the Church and the ecclesiastical censures under foot; and that he has resolutely persisted in scandalising Christians by his obstinacy in appealing to Jesus Christ, as to a sovereign judge, without employing the ecclesiastical ways and means; and inserting in the said appeal things false, injurious, and scandalous, in contempt of the Apostolic See, the censures and the keys of the Church.

Therefore this sacred Synod, for the reasons above mentioned and many others, decrees that Jan Hus ought to be judged and condemned as a heretic, and does actually judge and condemn him by these presents [this document], and reproves his appeal as injurious, scandalous, and made in derision of the spiritual jurisdiction. But as it is apparent, from all the Synod has seen, heard, and known, that Jan Hus is stubborn and incorrigible, and that he will not return to the pale of the Holy Mother Church by abjuring the errors and heresies which he has publicly maintained and preached, the sacred Synod of Constance declares that the said Jan Hus ought to be deposed and degraded from the order of priesthood, and the other orders with which he shall happen to be vested, giving it in express charge to the reverend fathers in Christ the Archbishop of Milan, the Bishops of Feltre, Asti, Alexandria, Bangor, and Lavour, to perform the said degradation in the presence of the Synod, according to law.

Hus listened to the reading of this sentence on his knees, and from time to time he tried to protest against the accusations made against him. He was prevented from speaking by those near him. When the reading of the sentence was ended, he called God to witness that he was innocent, and prayed him to forgive his judges and accusers. This, however, was received with tokens of anger and mockery on the part of the Council.

The ceremony of degradation followed immediately after the sentence against him was pronounced. He was ordered to put on the priestly robes. This he did, uttering words recording the similar ceremony in the case of Christ. Thus when he put on the robe he said, 'They put a white garment on our Lord Jesus Christ when Herod delivered him to Pilate.' Finally, when he was fully dressed they asked him once more to recant. However, he, facing the people, denied having any desire to offend or lead astray the faithful by a hypocritical and wicked recantation, protesting at the same time his innocence.

Then he was forced to descend from his seat, and the bishops, taking the chalice from his hands, said, 'O cursed Judas, who having forsaken the counsel of peace art entered into that of the Jews, we take this chalice from thee in which is the blood of Jesus Christ.' With similar curses they took from him each of his vestments, and finally cut his hair in such manner as to conceal his tonsure. They then put a paper crown or mitre on his head in the form of a pyramid, about eighteen inches in height, on which were painted grotesque figures of devils, and the word 'Heresiarcha'—arch-heretic—and in this condition they devoted his soul to the devils in hell.

Execution at the stake

Unshaken even by this solemn anathema, Hus commended his soul to God, and said aloud that he was glad to wear this crown of infamy, for the love of him who had worn one of thorns. After all this, he was handed over to the secular arm. The emperor handed him to the custody of Ludwig III, the Elector Palatine, who delivered him to the magistrates of Constance. They in their turn ordered the public executioner to burn him, with all his clothes and everything he had on his person, even to his girdle, knife, and purse, with every penny in it.

Surrounded by the city constabulary, followed by armed men and an innumerable multitude of people, he was led through the streets of the city to the place of execution, passing on the way there the episcopal palace, where his books were being burnt. As he approached the place of execution, he fell on his knees and cried out, 'Lord Jesus, have mercy on me! Into thy hands, O God, I commend my spirit.' Then some of the people said aloud, 'What this man has done before we know not, but now we hear him put up excellent prayers to God.'

As he was about to address the people he was interrupted by the Elector Palatine, who ordered the executioners to proceed to do their duty. As he raised his eyes toward heaven, his paper mitre fell off. Hus smiled at this, but the soldiers put it on his head again, saying it must be burnt with the devils whom he served.

As they tied him to the stake his face was turned toward the east, but since it was not proper for a heretic to die looking in that direction they turned him round toward the west. As the wood was being piled up about him, the Elector Palatine made a final appeal to him to recant, only to receive the sublime answer, 'God is my witness, that I have never taught nor preached those things which have been falsely ascribed to me, and the chief aim of all my preaching, writing, and acts was that I might save men from sin. And today I am willing and glad to die for that truth of the gospel which I have taught, written, and preached.'

Immediately the executioner set fire to the faggots and, while the flames were rising higher and higher, Hus cried, 'O Christ, thou Son of the living God, have mercy upon us!' A second time he cried out, 'Thou Son of the living God, have mercy upon us!' but when for the third time he began to say, 'Thou who wast born of the Virgin Mary', a gust of wind blew the flames into his face, and while his lips still moved he gave up the ghost.

Memorial to Jan Hus, Prague

When the wood was all burnt, the body was still seen to be hanging to the stake by means of the chain. The executioners beat the stake and all that remained on it to the ground, piled up more wood upon it, and burnt the remains. The heart having fallen out of the body, they stuck it on a stick and held it in the fire until it was destroyed.

Every article of clothing was burnt in the same manner in order (as the Elector Palatine said) that the Bohemians might not have anything to keep as relics. Not only this, but the ashes were carefully gathered together with some of the earth where the stake had stood. These were loaded on a cart and carried to the neighbouring Rhine, where they were cast into the river, in order that not a speck of his dust might remain on earth. However, the spot remained holy ground to the Bohemians, who dug up the soil and carried it back to their native land as a precious relic.

Chapter 8

Jerome of Prague

We have followed the history of Hus so closely in the preceding pages, that we have left out of sight many important and interesting events that were closely connected with him and his teachings. His power did not cease with his life. As we have already shown that it was necessary to give a general view of reforming ideas throughout the Middle Ages in order to estimate him aright, so for the same reason we cannot close this brief account of his life with the description of his death. With Hus, it was especially true that the blood of the martyrs is the seed of the Church. During all the terrible events that occurred in Bohemia for a quarter of a century after his death, the spirit of Hus was the leading influence, and lent unity to the whole movement of the Bohemian Reformation.

Jerome's trial at Constance

Before discussing the Hussite Wars, however, a word or two must be devoted to the fate of Hus's friend and fellow reformer, Jerome of Prague. We have seen how he came to Constance, how he hastily departed, and was captured and brought back as a prisoner. Before Hus's condemnation, Jerome had already undergone an examination before the Council. Amid cries of 'To the stake with him!' he defended his opinions with eloquence and force.

That night Petr z Mladoňovic knocked at the window of Jerome's prison, and cried out, 'Be steadfast, and fear not to die for the truth, concerning which you said such noble things when you were free.' To which Jerome answered: 'In truth, brother, I do not fear death, and as we once have said many things concerning the truth, we shall now see how it works in practice.'

Jerome's recantation

Alas for poor human nature! Jerome's glory was not destined to shine with the same pure, unsullied lustre of Hus. Worn out by sickness, his spirit broken by long confinement in chains, and intimidated by threats, he was forced to recant in his third hearing before the Council, on 11th September 1415. He signed a document in which he submitted to the will of the Council and approved the condemnation of Wycliffe and Hus.

Jerome's repentance

During the long months of prison life that followed, a change came over Jerome. His courage reasserted itself and a feeling of bitter remorse took possession of him. Hence, when he was brought again before the Council on 30th May 1416, he gave a marvellous exhibition of lofty courage and extraordinary eloquence and power.

A striking witness to the power of speech is that scene where, surrounded by hostile men, confronted by all the power, dignity, and learning of Christendom, Jerome made a public withdrawal of his former recantation. So nobly did he speak that Poggio

Bracciolini[101] said, 'Everybody was touched to the quick and wished he might escape.'

He declared that he had done nothing in his whole life that he ever repented of as bitterly as he did his recantation. He asserted that he revoked it from his very soul, that he had lied like a miscreant in making that recantation, and that Jan Hus was a holy man. In addition, when he was threatened with punishment if he did not repent, he is said to have made this prophetical answer, 'You have resolved to condemn me maliciously and unjustly, without having convicted me of any crime, but after my death I will leave a sting in your conscience and a worm that shall never die. I make my appeal from hence to the sovereign Judge of all the earth, in whose presence you shall appear to answer me a hundred years hence.'

Death sentence

After this, there was nothing more for the Council to do except to proceed to sentence Jerome to the same death that Hus had suffered. The story of his martyrdom is even more inspiring than that of his master, Hus. He seemed anxious to make amends for his former weakness by now maintaining a brave and unruffled demeanour. When they gave him a paper mitre with the devils painted upon it, similar to that given to Hus, Jerome cast his hat among the priests that surrounded him, and put the mitre on his head with his own hands, saying he was glad to wear it for the sake of him who was crowned with

---

[101] Gian Francesco Poggio Bracciolini (1380–1459), known as Poggio Bracciolini, was an Italian scholar. He was responsible for rediscovering and recovering a great number of classical Latin manuscripts from monastic libraries.

thorns. As the soldiers led him through the streets to the place of execution, he sang the Apostle's Creed and the hymns of the Church in a loud voice and with a cheerful countenance.

Execution at the stake

When he came to the place where Hus had been executed, Jerome knelt down before the stake and made a long prayer in a low voice. Then while he was being stripped and bound to the stake, and the wood was piled up about him, he raised his voice and sang the hymn, 'Salve festa dies toto venerabilis ævo / Qua Deus infernum vicit et astra tenens.'[102]

Jerome repeated the Apostles' Creed and then he addressed the multitude, and said, 'Dear friends, know that even as I have now sung, so do I believe, and not otherwise.' When fire was set to the wood, he cried out in Latin, 'Lord, into thy hands I commend my spirit.' And when he was almost smothered by the flame he cried out in Bohemian, 'O, Lord God Almighty, have mercy on me and pardon my transgressions, for thou knowest that I have sincerely loved thy truth.' And with these words he gave up the ghost.

Many writers of the times bear witness to the firmness with which Jerome met his death. Æneas Sylvius, who afterward became Pope Pius II, said, 'Hus was burnt first, and after him Jerome of Prague. They suffered death with very great constancy, and went to the fire as cheerfully as if it had been to a feast, without making any complaint. We do not find that any of the philosophers ever suffered death with so much constancy.' In a

---

[102] Hail, thou festive, ever venerable day / whereon hell is conquered and heaven is won by Christ!

letter written to Leonardo Bruni,[103] Poggio Bracciolini speaks of
Jerome's eloquence and constancy:

> I confess that I have never heard any person, in the defence of
> a criminal cause, who came nearer to that eloquence of the an-
> cients, which we admire every day, and when the executioners
> came from behind to light the fire he cried out, 'Come forward
> and set fire to it before my face. For had I been afraid, I should
> not have come hither when I might so easily have avoided it.'
> Thus died a man whose merit cannot be sufficiently admired. I
> was a witness of his end, and have considered all the acts.
> Whether he was guilty of insincerity or obstinacy, I know not,
> but never was there a death more philosophical.

---

[103] An Italian humanist, historian and statesman, often recognised as
the most important humanist historian of the early Renaissance. He
has been called the first modern historian.

Chapter 9

The Hussite Wars

With the execution of Jerome, we must leave the city of Constance and turn our eyes back to Bohemia, where the influence of Hus remained supreme, even after his death.

During his absence in Constance one question had grown up that was destined to play a very important role in the whole Hussite movement. In early times, it had been customary to present both the wafer and the cup to the laity during the celebration of the Eucharist. This custom, however, had gradually been given up in most countries entirely, and in Bohemia to some extent.

Strife about the chalice

A bitter strife arose in Bohemia over the question of the chalice. This was led by Jakoubek ze Stříbra. Through his influence, the custom of giving the cup or chalice spread throughout nearly all Bohemia, in spite of the fact that the Council of Constance solemnly condemned his doctrine. It was undoubtedly an additional cause for hatred toward Hus that the leaders of this movement for the Eucharist in two kinds were among his followers. Although he had nothing to do with starting the movement, he himself had written a letter from his prison endorsing the doctrine of Jacobellus (Jakoubek ze Stříbra).

Reaction to the martyrdom of Hus and Jerome

The attitude of the Council on this question was in itself enough to cause a wide rift between the Bohemians and the Roman Catholic Church. Yet this was nothing to the feeling stirred up by the treatment of Hus and Jerome in Constance, a feeling that rose to a veritable fury when both men were slain. Neither the Council nor the king seemed to be fully aware of the seriousness of the situation. At the news of Hus's death, the nobles had met in Bethlehem Chapel, had decreed honours of martyrdom to Hus, and sent a letter of protest to the Council, signed by sixty of the most distinguished men of the land.

The spirit of indignation shown in this protest letter gives us a clear idea of the state of mind that pervaded all Bohemia, and explains the long and wonderfully successful contests that the followers of Hus maintained against the Roman Catholic Church and its defender, Emperor Zikmund.

As by the laws of God and nature, everyone should do to others as he would that they should do to him, and as we ought not to do that to others which we would not that they should do to us; after reflection upon that divine maxim of love to our neighbour, we have thought fit to write these letters to you touching the Reverend Master Jan Hus, regular Bachelor of Divinity and Preacher of the Gospel. Meantime we know not from what motive you first condemned him in the Council of Constance, and then put him to a cruel and ignominious death as an obstinate heretic, without his having made any confession, or being convicted of any error or heresy, upon the false and sinister accusations of his capital [greatest] enemies, and the enemies of our kingdom, and of the Marquisate of Moravia, and by the instigation and importunity of certain traitors, to the eternal scandal of our most Christian Kingdom of Bohemia and to us all.

We protest, therefore, with the heart as well as the lips, that Master Jan Hus was a man very honest, just, and catholic; that for many years he conversed among us with godliness void of offence. That during all that time he explained to us and our subjects the Gospel and the books of the Old and New Testaments, according to the exposition of the holy doctors approved by the Church; and that he has left writings behind him, wherein he constantly abhors all error and all heresy, as he taught us to detest them, exhorting us at the same time, without ceasing, to peace and charity, and persuading us to it by both his discourses and example. So that we cannot find, after all the inquiry we have made, that the said Master Jan Hus ever taught or preached any error or heresy whatsoever, or that he offended any of us or our subjects in word or deed. On the contrary, he has lived with piety and good conduct, exhorting all mankind to the observation of the gospel and of the maxims of the holy fathers for the edification of Holy Mother Church and of our neighbours.

You are not content with disgracing us and our kingdom of Bohemia by these undertakings, but you have unmercifully imprisoned, and perhaps already put to death, Master Jerome of Prague, who certainly was a torrent of eloquence. Besides this, we have heard to our very great sorrow that certain slanderers, hateful to God and men, treacherous enemies to the kingdom of Bohemia, have wickedly and falsely reported to you and your Council that in the said kingdom several errors were propagated which had infected us and many others of the faithful.

We make known to you, Fathers, by these presents and also to all Christian people, with a firm confidence in Jesus Christ, attended with a pure and sincere conscience and an orthodox faith, that whosoever of any rank, pre-eminence, dignity, degree or religion whatsoever he be, has said and affirmed, or doth say and affirm, that errors and heresies are propagated in the kingdom of Bohemia, has told a capital lie, as a villain and traitor, the only dangerous heretic and a child of the devil, who is a liar and a murderer. And notwithstanding all that has passed, we are resolved to sacrifice our lives for the defence of the law of Jesus Christ and of his faithful preachers, who declare it with zeal, humility, and constancy, without being shocked by all human constitutions that shall oppose this resolution.

To this letter the Council replied on 23rd February 1416, summoning the signatories to Constance—a citation, however, which they did not obey.

Hussite factions

Finally the gauge of war was cast. On the one side stood the Roman Catholic Church with its powerful hierarchy, supported by the Emperor Zikmund; on the other stood practically the whole Bohemian nation, for by this time not only the upper classes, but even the peasants, had become followers of the martyred Hus.

If the Bohemians had only agreed among themselves, they might have finally succeeded in forming a national Church, or might even have anticipated by a hundred years the great Reformation. Alas, differences of opinion on matters of belief, as well as of politics, separated them into several distinct groups almost from the beginning. Before we can understand the trend matters took in Bohemia for the next quarter of a century, it is necessary for us to get some idea of these different groups and of the men who led them.

It is not to our purpose to speak of the loyal Roman Catholics. They formed in the beginning a very small minority, and constantly kept plotting against the Hussites, and especially did all they could to sow discord among them.

Calixtines and Taborites

The followers of Hus may be divided into two great divisions, the Calixtines (sometimes called Utraquists), and the Taborites.[104] The Calixtines were the conservative party, whose chief tenet was the use of the cup or chalice by the laity. There were various shades among them, some approaching very nearly to the Roman Catholics, and others not easy to distinguish from the Taborites. Despite their differences, both they and the Taborites all remained faithful to the end to the famous articles, which were for them the irreducible minimum in all negotiations with the Emperor Zikmund and others for all the years to come.

These Four Articles are as follows:
1. The demand that the Eucharist should be administered in two kinds—*i.e.*, that communicants should receive the chalice of wine as well as the wafer.

2. That the free preaching of the gospel should be allowed.

---

[104] In 1420, two men from the most radical wing of the Hussites founded a town named Tábor after the biblical Mount Tabor. Their followers soon became known as the Taborites. The town was built on an isolated hill, separated from the surrounding country by a river and an extensive lake, to which the Hussites gave the biblical name of Jordan. Tábor lies 48 miles (77 km) south of Prague.

3. That the punishment of public sins should be without privilege of the clergy.

4. That the temporal property of priests and religious institutions should be administered by the civil authorities.

The party of the Calixtines was composed of the leading men of Bohemia, and was largely recruited from the upper classes. The vast majority of the common people, however, belonged to the radical party, or Taborites, as they were called, from the newly organised city of Tábor, which was built by them, and which remained the centre of their religious and political life during all the years in which they still existed as an organised body.

Sects among the Taborites

We must by no means think of the Taborites as a compact and harmonious party, however. In it were gathered together all those who started out from Hus's doctrines and carried them to radical extremes along both social and political lines. What happens in all times of great revolutions among the people happened now. All the strange, mystic, extravagant, and superstitious doctrines, that had flourished among the Cathars and Waldensians, and that were to flourish later in the sects that swarmed through all Europe during the Reformation, then showed themselves among the Taborites.

Among them I may mention briefly the Picards,[105] the Nicolaites[106] and the Millenarians. The Millenarians believed that the

---

[105] A Hussite sect which lived in a communistic society. They rejected marriage and held wives in common, and also abolished distinctions of rank and riches. Žižka sent a force of 400 men to exterminate a group of Picards in 1421.

end of the world was at hand, that the old dreams of the Italian heretic, Gioacchino da Fiore, were about to come true—namely, that a new era of peace and holiness was to appear on the earth, when there should be no more sin or selfishness, when all men should be free and equal. They also believed that all distinctions between nobles and peasants would be wiped out, property would be abolished, labour would be unnecessary, and hunger and poverty would be unknown. As all men would become holy then, there should no longer be any need for the Bible or churches or creeds.

Those who believed in the speedy end of the world sold their property to prepare for the coming of the Lord, and strange individuals rose here and there proclaiming themselves to be Moses or Christ. The so-called Adamites[107] went so far as to preach the doctrine of having all things in common, even extending to having families and wives in common. Against these half-insane enthusiasts, however, the Taborite leader Žižka arose. With the same unrelenting cruelty he used towards all his enemies, soon practically all of the sects were destroyed in battle or by execution.

The mainstream Taborites

The real party of the Taborites, however, was composed of men who were more reasonable than Žižka. While despising the radical extremes of the Adamites and Picards, they likewise despised

---

[106] The errors of this sect are not specified. Various groups in history were labelled with this term, which refers to the Nicolaitans (Revelation chapter 2).

[107] A sect of the Taborites. They emulated the licentious behaviour of the original Adamites, a North African sect of the 3rd and 4th centuries.

the lukewarmness of the Calixtines, who at all times showed a willingness to make peace with the emperor and the Roman Catholic Church on the basis alone of the Four Articles.

The Taborites were uncompromising, and prepared themselves for the inevitable struggle that they foresaw was soon to come. They accepted the Four Articles as the Calixtines did, but in addition they discarded most of the ritual and the ancient customs of the Roman Catholic Church. They declared that Christ was the only lawgiver, and that his Word is sufficient to teach us what that law is. They ruthlessly swept away all the accumulated debris of the ages, and on the ruins of the papal and ecclesiastical power they raised a new Church, based on the authority solely of two things—the Bible and the human conscience.

Thus we see that the Calixtines were but little different from the orthodox Roman Catholics, retaining all their dogmas, the seven sacraments, invocation of the saints, worship of the Virgin Mary, and the doctrine of transubstantiation. In contrast, the Taborites were almost Protestants, keeping only two sacraments, those of baptism and the Lord's Supper. In addition, they denied the 'real presence' in the bread and wine, and condemned the worship of relics and the invocation of the saints.

The two parties naturally differed in the outer forms. The Calixtines kept all Roman Catholic services and observances, whereas the Taborites abolished feasts and fasts, dissolved monasteries and convents, and repudiated sumptuous vestments and all the pomp and ceremony of the mass. While they did not definitely declare that every layman was a priest, they did show themselves utterly indifferent to all external signs as well as the tonsure, priestly costume, and so on, which marked out the priests from other men. According to the Taborites, every man who followed Christ could teach and preach, even without the permission of the bishop.

The customs and manners of the Taborites were very much like those of the Puritans in the days of Cromwell. Indeed, there is a striking resemblance between these two peoples, rising in the name of religion and waging war under the standard of the Prince of Peace. The manner of life of the army of the Taborites was ascetic to a degree: the discipline was entirely based on religion. All trivial amusements were forbidden—no cards or dice, no dancing or even music were allowed. The children were taught to read at an early age, and the entire people were ruled by the Bible. Æneas Sylvius blushed when he saw that, while many priests had never read the New Testament, even a number of the Taborite women knew the whole Bible.

It is interesting to read the picture of the life of these people as given by Æneas Sylvius, who was one of several ambassadors sent to negotiate with them at their headquarters in Tábor.

> A most remarkable spectacle was now witnessed, an indiscriminate rabble, mostly composed of peasants. Although a cold rainstorm prevailed at the time, they had no other protection than a mere frock. Some wore robes made of skins. Some of their horsemen had no saddles, some had no bridles, and others were without stirrups. One was booted, another not. Having entered the town, we took a view of it, and if I were not to call it a town or asylum for heretics, I should be at a loss for a name to give it. On the outer gate of the city there are two shields hung suspended. On one of these is a picture of an angel holding a cup, which he is represented as extending to the people as if to invite them to share in the communion. On the other,

there is a portrait of Žižka, who is represented as an old man and entirely blind. These people have no greater anxiety for anything than to hear a sermon. Their place of worship is built of wood, and is much like a barn: this they call their temple.

Jan Žižka

One of the most curious things in all this strange, eventful history is the character of the leaders of the Hussites, especially the Taborites. Hus himself was a man of gentle, conciliating disposition, was by no means endowed with great executive ability, and felt a spirit of love and kindliness towards even his bitterest enemies. The leader of the forces of the Bohemians, when the inevitable struggle finally broke forth, was in many respects more like Attila the Hun, 'the scourge of God', than like the man whose doctrines he maintained against mighty armies, by means of fire and sword. Legend has told repeatedly of his cruelty, his thirst for vengeance, and his untiring sternness toward his enemies.

Jan Žižka z Trocnova[108] [John Žižka of Trocnov] is generally known simply by his surname Žižka. He belonged to the common people, and it was this fact undoubtedly that helped to give him his extraordinary popularity. He was a man of middle height, with broad shoulders, thick lips, and closely cropped hair, with a long black moustache, after the Polish fashion.

His strange appearance was heightened by the fact that he only had one eye. Later he lost this eye too, so that his last campaigns were carried on while he was totally blind. Two sentiments filled him with inflexible passion—patriotism and faith in Hussitism. As Palacký says, 'He was a fanatic and had the unshakable con-

---

[108] Pronounced Yan Zheeshka Strotsnova.

viction of fanaticism, its intolerance, and its unpitying and inflexible logic.'

Memorial to Žižka, Tábor

Žižka was a military genius of the highest order, and it was undoubtedly due almost entirely to him that the Bohemians never lost a battle, during all those long years of contest with nearly all Christendom. Having no horses, he was unable to fight with the usual means of warfare at that time, and was forced to rely entirely on infantry. He made his foot soldiers so formidable, however, that his army became the object of almost superstitious terror on the part of his enemies. Moved by one common impulse, in perfect discipline and order, wielding long poles, fifteen to eighteen feet in length, armed with iron points—it was only later that they had guns and cannon—they all marched together, men, women, and even children, toward the enemy, whom they invariably put to flight.

One invention of Žižka especially proved successful, the moving ramparts formed of wagons bound together by chains and protected by boards, behind which the shooters were hidden. On the march, these wagons proceeded in rows of twos and fours, each one carrying twenty men. However, when the battle was fought, they swung around into position and formed a barricade, which all the efforts of the enemy were never able to scale. Such was the perfect instrument of warfare of Žižka, and long after his death it proved its invincibility in the hands of his successors, the Taborite generals Prokop Holý and Prokop Malý [Prokop the Great and Prokop the Lesser].

The first anti-Hussite crusade

It is not our place here to consider in detail the terrible wars that swept over Bohemia for a quarter of a century after the death of Hus. And yet we must cast at least a fleeting glance at the main currents of these movements, which were often of truly epic grandeur. We have seen how wide the cleft had grown between the Roman Catholic Church and Bohemia after the events at Constance, which culminated in the deaths of Jan Hus and Jerome. For some time, however, events stood still, although low mutterings continued to be heard along the horizon from time to time.

The first impulse to open hostilities occurred only when Pope Martin sent a legate to execute the decree of the Council and his own Bull. The legate was driven out of the country by the enraged people, who now flocked from all sides to the standard raised by Žižka. At this crucial moment in 1419, King Václav died, and another question, that of the naming of a successor, came to complicate matters. There was still a large number of conservatives, who hoped that by electing Zikmund Lucemburský to the throne they might make favourable conditions for their own faith. If Zikmund had been a wise man, he would have seen how matters lay. However, he was strong in his own self-confidence, and he treated with contempt all negotiations based on the Four Articles, declaring he would govern Bohemia as his father Karel IV had done—that is, he would make no compromise with heresy.

After this uncompromising attitude on the part of Zikmund, nothing stood in the way of a bitter civil war. In answer to the desire of King Zikmund, Pope Martin V issued a bull on 1st March 1420, in which he invited all Christendom to seize arms, march toward Bohemia, and help to destroy the Wycliffites, Hussites, and all other heretics, promising full indulgences to all those who would either take part themselves or would pay for a substitute. The effect of the bull throughout all Europe was extraordinary: volunteers to join the Bohemian king's forces flowed in from all lands, Poland, Germany, France, England, and even Spain. The army finally under Zikmund's orders is said to have amounted to one hundred and forty thousand or one hundred and fifty thousand men.

In the meantime, the approaching danger united all parties of the Hussites in defence of their faith. Although a number of cities fell into the hands of the king, the followers of Hus made their way to Prague, where the final and decisive combat was to take place. The city was surrounded and besieged, but owing to the generalship of Žižka and the heroic conduct of the Hussites, especially the Taborites, all efforts to take the city were in vain. After many defeats and disasters, the imperial army was forced to abandon the siege and retreat. Thus ended what is known as the First Crusade of the Bohemian wars.

The second anti-Hussite crusade

Bohemia now became the most prominent country in all Christendom. The teachings of Hus spread through all lands, while the quasi-socialistic and republican doctrines of the Taborites threatened to undermine the very basis of political authority in Europe. This fact was skilfully taken advantage of by the pope in preaching a new crusade, for he pointed out that not only ecclesiastical but also monarchical institutions were at stake.

A second invasion was organised. Two hundred thousand men marched toward Bohemia, and laid siege to Žatec, one of the 'holy cities' of the Taborites.[109] Although this city had a garrison numbering only five or six thousand, it repulsed all assaults, and waited in confidence for the arrival of reinforcements. The besieging army in the meantime lost all discipline, and spent their time in foraging the country, burning villages, and slaying every man, woman, or child that spoke Bohemian, irrespective of their religious beliefs. The Hussites set out from Prague to assist their compatriots who were shut up in Žatec. Before they could reach the city, however, the undisciplined mob of mercenaries, which formed the imperial army, took fright at the approach of the dreaded Taborite hordes and fled. They were pursued by the garrison of Žatec, who slew thousands in their flight. This took place in October 1421.

While this imperial army fled back towards Germany, the emperor himself with eighty thousand men invaded Moravia.[110]

---

[109] Žatec (pronounced Zhatets) is a Bohemian town, 43 miles (70 km) northwest of Prague.
[110] One of the historical 'Czech lands', together with Bohemia and Czech Silesia. It forms the eastern part of the present Czech Republic.

Here Žižka's genius manifested itself in its full power. By rapidity of movement, by skilful choice of field of battle, by ingenious strategy, by untiring diligence, he won a complete victory over his imperial adversary. On 21st December 1421, he was attacked in an open plain, but he made a rampart of carts and repulsed all assaults. He himself left to seek reinforcements, and on his return, on 6th January 1422, he attacked the enemy, cut their army in two, and so confused the emperor that the latter lost his nerve and turned to flight, followed hotly by the Taborites. Many thousands were slain or perished of cold and hunger. In four days of combat, Žižka won three battles, took two fortified cities, slew twelve thousand men, and made many thousands prisoners. Thus the Second Crusade ended as the first, in complete disaster to the Roman Catholic arms.

The third anti-Hussite crusade

In July 1422, another crusade against the Hussites was ordered by the Diet of Nürnberg. The army was under the command of Friedrich I [Frederick of Brandenburg], but being deserted by the emperor, he accomplished but little.

Death of Žižka and its consequences

An event now occurred which meant more to the Hussites than the loss of many battles, namely the death of Žižka. The background to this event was dissension between the various Hussite factions. As soon as the foreign enemies had left Bohemia in peace for a short period, discord and bitter animosity filled the ranks of the Hussites. The differences in religious, social, and political views between the Calixtines and the Taborites were too deep to be easily reconciled. While they all agreed on the Four Articles, they differed fundamentally on nearly every other point. Once the Germans retreated, anarchy broke forth in Bohemia, and so bitter became the quarrels between the hostile parties that it seemed as if war alone could settle their difference.

At the head of the Calixtines was Zikmund Korybutovič[111] [Sigismund Korybut]; at the head of the Taborites was Žižka. The Calixtines prepared to defend Prague against the Taborites; but when Žižka with his terrible army approached, the terror-stricken citizens of Prague sent a mission headed by Jan Rokycana[112] [John of Rokycany] to beg Žižka to save the city. The Taborites considered Prague to be a holy city, and they forced their leader, Žižka, to conclude a peace treaty. He did this unwillingly and with a saddened heart, for he knew it was only putting off the inevitable conflict. Soon after, he was stricken with the plague, and died on 11th October 1424.

His death filled the whole army with profound sorrow and desolation. He was buried at Čáslav,[113] and near his tomb was placed this inscription: 'O Hus! Here lies Jan Žižka, your avenger, and the emperor himself has bent before him.' It is said that more than a century afterwards the Emperor Ferdinand was passing through the country, and saw a mass of iron hanging near a tomb. He asked his courtiers to read the inscription, but they dared not repeat it to him, so he approached and read himself the name of Žižka. 'Fie, Fie!' said he. 'This ugly beast, dead a hundred years, still frightens the living.' Yet, although Ferdinand had intended to pass the night in the city, he changed his mind and proceeded on his way.

---

[111] Pronounced Zikmunt Korybutovitsh.
[112] Pronounced Yan Rockytsana.
[113] Pronounced Tshaslaf. A town in the eastern part of Central Bohemia, 45 miles (72 km) southeast of Prague.

With the death of Žižka, the Taborites had lost the one man who had held together the various elements of which they were composed. They now fell asunder, and in addition to the regular Taborites, some formed a new party, called the Orphans[114] (alluding to the death of Žižka), which were similar to the Calixtines in their religious beliefs, and similar to the Taborites in their social ideas. They had their separate chiefs and a separate capital; in general, however, they sided with the Taborites.

With the death of Žižka, the first period of the Hussite Wars ended. The Bohemians had become a powerful nation and had held in check the efforts of all Christendom marshalled against them. They had shown the world that they were a power not to be despised. It is not necessary here to give in detail all the events that followed—the skirmishes and battles at home and abroad, the constant quarrels and discord that rent the body of Hussites, and slowly prepared the dissolution that was to come.

Prokop Holý

In the first few years after Žižka's death, it seemed as if the nation was as strong as ever. It is true that the new Commander-in-chief, Prokop Holý, was not so great an organiser as Žižka, but he had a great many of the latter's extraordinary qualities as a general and strategist. He found a veteran army made ready to his hand, hardened and trained by many years of warfare and discipline, and rendered confident in its invincibility by a series of victories that was not broken by a single defeat. This army

---

[114] The Orphans originated in eastern Bohemia. They were originally named Orebites from taking part in a procession on a low mountain called Oreb. They were renamed Orphans in an allusion to the death of the Hussite commander, Žižka, whom they esteemed as their 'father'.

was used by Prokop with distinguished ability: he had the same rapidity of movement, surety of glance, and boldness of attack that had been so characteristic of Žižka.

Memorial to Prokop Holý, Český Brod

The whole aim of Prokop was to bring peace and tranquillity once more to his native land. He soon foresaw that the best way to accomplish this aim was not to wait patiently within the frontiers of Bohemia until the enemy could raise an army and attack him, but rather to inspire fear and respect in the hearts of those countries in which the various crusades had been recruited. He hoped by ravaging these countries to direct their attention from Bohemia to their own territories, and thus possibly he might be able to make a lasting treaty of peace.

After having defeated a large army of the imperial allies near the city of Ústí nad Labem[115] in northern Bohemia, and after having restored a short-lived peace among the discordant elements of the Hussites, Prokop undertook to carry out his plan of foreign invasion in 1427. Since the disgraceful failure of the third crusade in 1422, Germany had nearly forgotten her humiliation, but she was suddenly brought to a realising sense of the dangerous condition of the neighbouring country of Bohemia, by the news of a large army of Hussites. Prokop's forces had crossed the frontiers of their native land and were ravaging Austria, Moravia, and Silesia.

The fourth anti-Hussite crusade

An Imperial Diet was hastily summoned in April 1427, and it was resolved to attack Bohemia with four armies at four different points. Friedrich I von Brandenburg once more organised the war against the Hussites.

The commander-in-chief of the combined forces was the Cardinal Legate Henry of Winchester, half-brother of Henry IV of England, and uncle of the Dukes of Bedford and Gloucester. The army in all was not far from two hundred thousand men, about equally divided between infantry and cavalry. They started out, full of hope and confidence, they captured cities, laid waste the country, and everywhere acted with their customary licentious behaviour and lack of discipline. Against this huge army of mercenaries, the Calixtines, Taborites, and Orphans—once more united, as they always had been when foreign enemies

---

[115] Pronounced Oostee nad Lahbem. A city in northern Bohemia, close to the present border with Germany. It is located on the River Labe, which becomes the Elbe in Germany.

came to threaten their native land—opposed a solid front of well-trained, well-disciplined, and well-seasoned veterans.

The Hussite forces marched toward Stříbro, where the enemy was encamped. Scarcely had the Germans heard the noise of the approaching Hussites, when the old panic seized them once more, and they fled before the enemy had even come within sight. They were met by Cardinal Winchester—he was arriving with reinforcements and succeeded in checking their flight. He induced them to turn back and meet the Bohemians, who were far inferior in numbers. However, as soon as they saw the ranks of the Taborites, they were again seized with panic, and fled in an irresistible wave of retreat, which swept everything along with it.

Rendered still more confident by this victory, Prokop in the following year carried on that extraordinary campaign throughout the various lands of Germany that filled the hearts of all men with terror and dismay. All branches of Hussites supported him, and took part in these expeditions—Calixtines as well as Orphans and Taborites. Bands of soldiers were sent to Silesia, Saxony, Bavaria, and even to France. They captured great cities, burned villages, and everywhere left behind them death and desolation.

The fifth anti-Hussite crusade

All Germany was aroused to desperate efforts to meet this danger. The German princes gathered an army of one hundred thousand men, nearly four times the size of the Bohemian forces, which never amounted to more than thirty thousand. Zikmund, who had been busy fighting the Turks in Eastern Europe, now came back after many years of absence from Germany. The Diet of Nürnberg, held in February 1431, ordered a new crusade, which was preached by Pope Eugene IV, the successor of Martin V.

A vast number of men advanced towards the frontiers of Bohemia. The general command was in the hands of the Elector Friedrich von Brandenburg. Yet they had no general plan of action; they entered Bohemia, devastated the fields and massacred the peasants. No one was spared, not even the Catholics. They stopped, however, at the news of the approach of the Hussites. On 14th August 1431, toward three o'clock in the afternoon, they heard the noise of the chariots of war, and the hymns sung by the Taborites. The old scenes repeated themselves: a wild terror seized the whole army. The emperor's forces flung away their arms and all other impediments and they turned to a mad flight, leaving behind them thousands of slain, and an immense quantity of booty for the Hussite forces.

Council of Basel

Now all parties began to see the uselessness of these bloody contests, which led to no decisive results. It was no longer a question of Bohemia alone. All Europe was involved in the mighty upheaval. The ideas of the Hussites were scattered far and wide. One of their manifestos was even found nailed to the door of the Church of Basel, where the Ecumenical Council of Basel was in session in 1431.[116] The manifesto had been written

---

[116] This is also known as the Council of Basel-Ferrara-Florence, as it began in Basel in 1431, was moved to Ferrara in 1438, and continued in Florence from 1439 until 1449. It was the Seventeenth Ecumenical Council of the Roman Catholic Church, and was convoked by Pope Martin V shortly before his death. It took place in the context of the Hussite Wars in Bohemia and the rise of the Ottoman Empire.

by Prokop, and it produced an immense impression. Everywhere in Germany revolts among the peasantry occurred, and leagues were organised. A cry for peace arose throughout all Europe, and the pope was implored to make all concessions that were not inconsistent with the very existence of the Roman Catholic Church.

On the other hand, Bohemia was utterly exhausted—the land was a desert and countless villages were depopulated. Although the Bohemians had invariably been victorious, multitudes had been slain. Hence when the Council of Basel invited the Hussites to send delegates with a view to coming to some agreement on the subjects under dispute, all the Hussite parties finally agreed to send a delegation after some hesitation. It included Prokop Holý, leader of the Taborites, and Rokycana, head of the Calixtine party.

> It was with strange feelings that the inhabitants of Basel, as well as those who had come to attend the Council, awaited the entry of these men, whose names had become legendary throughout Europe. In the words of Æneas Sylvius (quoted by Palacký): They streamed into the streets; women and children looked out of the windows and pointed out with their fingers the different members of the party, gazing with wonder at their strange costume, stern faces, and wild eyes. The eyes of most, however, were fastened on Prokop; he was the one who so often had destroyed the vast armies of the faithful [Roman Catholics] and slain so many thousands, feared by friends as well as enemies, as an unconquered, bold, restless general, undismayed in the face of any danger.

Disagreement between Hussite factions

It is not the place here to discuss the complicated negotiations that followed—the hopes and fears, the doubts and disgust of the Hussites—as soon as it became manifest that a satisfactory solution was not yet to be. The Hussites left Basel on 14th April 1433. The Council sent a commission to Prague, but it did little more than secretly to sow the seeds of discord among the various parties of the Hussites. These discords, which had existed from the very beginning, now began to assume proportions so great that the only outcome was war between them. On the one hand, the Calixtines, supported by the nobles, were finally agreed to accept the compromise proposed by the Council of Basel. The compromise pretended to yield to the demands of the Hussites that the Four Articles should be respected. In reality, it left a loophole of escape on the part of the Roman Catholic Church as soon as its strength and the weakness of the Hussites would permit. On the other hand, the Taborites and Orphans, led by Prokop, opposed uncompromisingly the acceptance of the Compacts of Basel, or *Compactata*, as the compromise was called in Latin.

The last battle of the Hussite Wars

Now Prague was in the hands of the reactionary Calixtine nobles. Prokop set out with his army to lay siege to them. The nobles with twenty-five thousand men met him near Lipany,[117] where the final battle of the great Hussite Wars was fought out to the bitter end—not this time a battle between the united party of Bohemians and a foreign enemy, but between different members of that party itself. For the first time the Taborites

---

[117] A village located 25 miles (40 km) east of Prague.

were defeated—sixteen thousand dead were left on the field of battle, among them being Prokop Holý himself.

Chapter 10

Conclusion

With the battle of Lipany and the death of Prokop, the Hussite movement came to an end for all practical purposes. What all the power of the papacy and the empire had not been able to do—that is, to destroy the teachings of Hus throughout Bohemia—was now accomplished by internal discord. Although Hussitism was not immediately crushed out, as (for instance) the Albigensians had been, yet for the next two hundred years we mark an ever-diminishing influence in Bohemia itself, until in the early eighteenth century the last vestiges disappeared forever from its native soil.

The aftermath of the Hussite Wars

For a long time the Hussites remained strong enough to make a compromise, and Emperor Zikmund himself accepted as the basis of the compromise the *Compactata*, the concordat between the Council of Basel and the States of Bohemia. The *Compactata* safeguarded in a certain sense the Four Articles, which had from first to last formed the irreducible minimum in all negotiations on the part of the Hussites. As we may naturally suppose, Emperor Zikmund paid no attention to the *Compactata*, which were formally abolished by Pope Pius II in 1462.

After the death of Zikmund in 1437, we have a succession of
kings of Bohemia most of whom we may pass over, merely
mentioning Jiří z Poděbrad[118] [George of Poděbrady] (who died
1471) and Vladislav Jagellonský[119] [Vladislaus II of Hungary],
whose reign and that of his son Ludvík Jagellonský [Louis II of
Hungary] mark the end of the political and religious independence of Bohemia. Anne, sister of Ludvík, who became heir to
the crown of Bohemia and Moravia by marrying Ferdinand of
Austria, grandson of Emperor Maximilian, brought these countries over to the House of Habsburg. After that, Bohemia
formed an integral part of the Austrian Empire.

The subsequent history of the Hussite factions

Such in brief outline is the political history of Bohemia in the
years immediately following the great events we have been considering. Its religious history is marked by melancholy interest.
The old bond of union between Calixtines and Taborites—
patriotism—was broken when Bohemia lost its freedom. The
two parties now developed in different ways.

After many vicissitudes, the Calixtines were either destroyed by
persecution, united with the Roman Catholics, or later merged
with the Lutherans. After the sixteenth century, all traces of
them disappeared forever. Not so the Taborites, however. Under another name and under changed beliefs they still exist, scattered far and wide over the world. Even in the midst of savage
warfare, many had fought only under necessity, and had longed
for a quiet and peaceful existence, devoted to the worship of
God and the service of suffering humanity. Now, when all their

---

[118] Pronounced Yeerzhee Spodyebrat.
[119] Pronounced Vladislaf Yagellonskee.

victories and all the terrible loss of life had apparently been in vain, the more gentle and spiritual among them turned from earthly to heavenly things. They adopted some of the doctrines of the Waldensians, and soon a large sect arose, called the Brethren, and later the United Brethren or Unity of the Brethren (known by the Latin name Unitas Fratrum).[120] The United Brethren then became the Moravian Church.

The Moravian Church

From this point on, tracing the influence of Hus involves the history of the Moravians. Their history affords a monotonous repetition of all persecuted sects—the same tale of slaughter and exile, brightened by the same examples of heroism and martyrdom, cheerfully accepted for the glory of God. They were persecuted in 1458, when Jiří z Poděbrad became king, and again in 1468 at the instigation of Rokycana. In 1523, they sent a commission to Luther to give an account of their doctrines and constitution, at which he was well pleased. In 1535, Luther and Melanchthon wrote to them (among other things) as follows: 'Since we are agreed in the principal articles of the Christian doctrine, let us receive one another in love; nor shall any difference of usages and ceremonies disunite our hearts.'

In 1546, after Luther's death, the Moravians refused to support Emperor Charles V and their own King Ferdinand against the Protestants, and they were accused of plotting to bring about the election of the Elector of Saxony to the Bohemian throne. From this arose a new outburst of persecution, during which their churches were closed and many were imprisoned or banished.

---

[120] They received episcopal ordination by the Waldensians in 1467.

The prospects of the Moravians seemed to brighten with the opening of the seventeenth century. In 1609, King Rudolf II [Rudolph II] ratified the free exercise of religion they had received under Maximilian II, and gave them the privilege of erecting churches and choosing nobles to protect their rights. The famous Bethlehem Chapel at Prague, in which Hus had preached, was handed over to them.

The Thirty Years' War

All this, however, was only a deceitful calm before the last dreadful tempest, which was soon to swoop down upon them with destructive fury. Rudolf died in 1612 and was succeeded by his brother Matyáš Habsburský[121] [Matthias of Habsburg], who was in turn succeeded by his cousin Ferdinand II Štýrský[122] [Ferdinand II of Styria]. By this time, the plan to persecute Protestants adopted by the Council of Trent had begun in Bohemia. The mass of the Protestant people were filled with rage. They renounced their allegiance to the new king, Ferdinand, and flung the imperial councillors out of a window of Prague Castle on 23rd May 1618, an event that has come to be known as the Second Defenestration of Prague.[123] They then elected Friedrich V (the Elector Palatine), son-in-law of James VI of Scot-

---

[121] Pronounced Matyash Habsburskee.

[122] Pronounced Ferdinand Shteerskee.

[123] Remarkably, the three officials survived the 70 foot (21 m) fall. (The First Defenestration of Prague occurred in 1419 when radical Hussites retaliated to an attack and stormed the New Town Hall in Prague. They killed seven members of the city council by throwing them from a window. Roman Catholic reaction to this precipitated the beginning of the five anti-Hussite crusades of the Hussite Wars.)

land and I of England,[124] as their king, and thus precipitated the contest known as the Thirty Years' War, which lasted from 1618 to 1648.[125]

The tide of warfare, however, soon rolled its waves far from them, leaving the last followers of Hus in Bohemia a prey to the terrible Roman Catholic persecutions that followed the disastrous defeat at Bílá Hora [White Mountain] near Prague, in 1620.[126] The Hussites were flung into prison, put to death, or

---

[124] King James (1566–1625) was the son of Mary, Queen of Scots. His daughter, Elizabeth Stuart (1596–1662) married Friedrich V at the Palace of Whitehall in 1613. Friedrich became king of Bohemia in November 1619. Friedrich abdicated after his defeat by Ferdinand at the Battle of Bílá Hora on 8th November 1620. Due to the brevity of her reign and to the season of the battle, Elizabeth is known as the Winter Queen.

[125] This began as a war in Central Europe between various Protestant and Catholic states within the Holy Roman Empire. Gradually it developed into a more general conflict involving most of the great powers of Europe. Possibly eight million died as a result of warfare, starvation and disease. The conflict was concluded by the Peace of Westphalia, a series of peace treaties signed in 1648 in the Westphalian cities of Osnabrück and Münster. The treaties effectively ended two European wars of religion—the Thirty Years' War (1618–1648) in the Holy Roman Empire and the Eighty Years' War (1568–1648) between Spain and the Dutch Republic.

[126] A Protestant Bohemian army was comprehensively defeated by the combined armies of Emperor Ferdinand II and the German Catholic League at Bílá Hora near Prague. The battle marked the end of the first (Bohemian) phase of the Thirty Years' War. It also dramatically changed the religious landscape of the Czech lands. After two centuries of Protestant dominance, militant Roman Catholicism swept to power. This had disastrous consequences for Bohemian Protestantism for the next three centuries. In 1621, the year after the Battle of Bílá Hora, the Emperor ordered all Calvinists and other non-Lutherans to leave the realm in three days or to convert to Roman Catholicism. In 1622, he prohibited the practice of the Lutheran faith, and in 1626, he

banished. Their ministers hid themselves in forests, lived on the mountains and in caves, and stealthily stole forth from time to time to visit their suffering flocks. Hundreds of the noble and wealthy families fled to Prussia, Poland, Silesia, and even as far as the Netherlands. Among the most illustrious of these exiles was Jan Amos Komenský [John Amos Comenius] (1592–1670), the famed educationalist and writer, whose reputation went so far as to bring him an invitation to become president of Harvard University.[127]

Hussites after the Thirty Years' War

Of the Hussites (mostly the common people) who remained in Bohemia, we know very little during the succeeding years. They were forced to conform to the Catholic Church. No doubt, a large number remained in it, but in the case of many, this conformity was merely external. After the end of the Thirty Years' War, they must have lost all hope, for they alone of all the Protestant bodies were not included in the terms of the Peace of Westphalia in 1648.

In the early part of the 18th century, after a long period of utter silence, we see once more (and for the last time) an active movement among the Brethren, or Moravians as they are better known to us now. In 1717, a large number left Bohemia and went to Upper Lusatia,[128] where they joined their compatriots

---

ordered all Lutherans to either convert or else to leave the country. By these aggressive measures, Roman Catholicism became and remained the majority religion in the Czech lands until the late 20th century.

[127] Harvard was founded in 1636.

[128] A historical region in Germany and Poland. The major part of Upper Lusatia belongs to the German state of Saxony, roughly comprising the Bautzen and Görlitz districts. By the middle of the 16th century

who already had settled there. Later Christian David, tutor to the Baron von Schweinitz, had a meeting with Count Zinzendorf, who was anxious for the salvation of the children of his subjects. The outcome of this and other conferences was the establishment of the village of Herrnhut, on the estate of Zinzendorf, which from that time on became the centre of the Moravian Church throughout the world.[129] From the very first, missions became an absorbing part of their work. From their desire to save the Native Americans, they established settlements in Georgia and especially in Pennsylvania. The town of Bethlehem in that state became the largest Moravian community in the world.[130]

Hus and his legacy

We have thus traced the life of Jan Hus in brief. We have tried to show his position as summing up certain evangelical doctrines that had been sporadically in the minds of men for centu-

---

about 90% of Bohemians were Protestant, and this led the Roman Catholic Habsburg rulers to instigate a counter-Reformation. Roman Catholic educational institutions were established through the activities of the Jesuits, and the persecuting policies of the Council of Trent were implemented. After the Thirty Years' War, the Protestant remnant in Bohemia was vigorously suppressed and numbers emigrated from Moravia to Upper Lusatia.

[129] A town in Saxony, Germany, near the borders of Poland and the Czech Republic. Zinzendorf founded the community of the Moravian Church on his estate near the town in 1772.

[130] Zinzendorf led a small group of Moravians to establish missionary communities in Pennsylvania among the Native Americans and unchurched German-speaking Christians. He founded the community of Bethlehem in December 1741. Missionary work by the Moravian Church has led to a large following, and current worldwide membership is around 750,000. The Church is strongly ecumenical, Arminian in doctrine, and episcopal in church government.

ries, and we have tried to show the vicissitudes of his followers down through the ages.

Yet the influence of Hus was not only exerted upon his immediate followers. Martin Luther himself tells how great that influence had been on the Reformation that he himself had set in motion: 'In my opinion Jan Hus bought with his own blood the gospel which we now possess.' His place in this world-shaking movement is well represented in a miniature picture in an old Moravian hymnbook preserved in the University Library at Prague, which represents Wycliffe seizing a torch, Hus lighting it, and Luther holding it on high.

Later the followers of Hus, scattered all over Christendom, had no small influence on the various forms of Protestantism. They gave a distinctly pietistic turn to religion in the eighteenth century. Zinzendorf, who was a Lutheran, soon became the leader of the Moravians, holding some such relation to them and the Lutheran Church as Wesley did to the Methodists and the Church of England. It is not too much to say that Methodism is largely the outcome of Moravianism. We never can know what might have happened if John Wesley had not met August Spangenberg in Georgia, and especially Peter Böhler in London. When he went to Herrnhut, where he spent two weeks with Zinzendorf, he was filled with devout enthusiasm and cried, 'Oh that this religion might cover the earth, as the waters cover the sea!'

The glory of Jan Hus is not confined to his influence on one religious denomination or another. His heroic death as a martyr witnessed to the truth of God. Because he was fortified by the breastplate of a clear conscience, none of the combined efforts of the Roman Catholic Church and the Holy Roman Empire could make him falter for a single moment. At the time, it seemed an unequal contest between this lonely man and the mighty concourse of his adversaries; at the time, it seemed as if he had ignominiously failed. However, we know better now. The proud and contemptuous hierarchy of Rome began to falter. Just over a century after the martyrdom of Jan Hus, the Lord raised up Martin Luther to make a stand for the truth, and that work of reformation continued with the labours of other men of God.

Appendix

Biographical notes

Mediaeval European personal names often consisted of a fore-name, the preposition 'of' or 'from', and the name of a town or village name denoting the place of birth or residence. The preposition can alternatively act as a 'nobiliary particle' indicating noble lineage. The book features people with equivalents of the prepositions 'of' or 'from' in Czech (z or ze), German (von or von der), French (d', de or de la) and Italian (di). The Czech prepositions alter the spelling of the place name.

Names are listed alphabetically according to the 'true' surname and hence (for example) Michal z Brodu appears among sur-names beginning with 'B', and the entry is 'z Brodu, Michal'. However, rulers and popes are listed in the traditional way by the regnal name (*e.g.*, Ferdinand I of Austria).

Abélard, Pierre [Peter Abelard] (1079–1142)
A French philosopher and theologian.

Æneas Sylvius Bartholomeus
See **Pius II**.

d'Ailly, Pierre (1351–1420)

French theologian, who was Chancellor of the University of Paris. Later he became Bishop of Noyon and then Cardinal of Cambrai. He was a formidable opponent of antipope John XIII at the Council of Constance, and also took a leading part in condemning the views of Jan Hus at the Council.

Alexander V (*c.* 1339–1410)

Born in Crete as Petros Philargos, but often known by the Italian form of his name, Pietro di Candia. During the Western Schism, he supported the 'official' pope, Urban VI. He was Archbishop of Milan when the Council of Pisa appointed him as Pope Alexander V in 1409. He reigned until his death in 1410 as a rival Pisan antipope to the 'official' Roman pope Gregory XII and the Avignon antipope Benedict XIII.

Amalric, Arnaud (died 1225)

A Cistercian abbot who played a prominent role in the crusade against the Albigensians in southern France. He became a papal legate and inquisitor in 1204. Pope Innocent III commissioned him to convert the Albigensians. Having failed to achieve this, Amalric led a crusade against them, including the sack of Béziers in 1209, which led to the indiscriminate slaughter of 20,000 inhabitants.

Anselm (c. 1033–1109)

Anselm was a theologian of the Catholic Church, who held the office of Archbishop of Canterbury from 1093 to 1109. He wrote with a rational and philosophical approach, and this has led to him being known as the founder of Scholasticism.

Aquinas, Thomas (1225–1274)

Italian Dominican friar, who was an influential scholastic theologian. He embraced several ideas of Aristotle and attempted to synthesise Aristotelian philosophy with the principles of Christianity.

Assisi, Francis of (1181/82–1226)

Born Giovanni di Pietro di Bernardone, and informally named as Francesco [Francis]. He was an Italian Roman Catholic friar, deacon and preacher, and founded the Order of Friars Minor, the women's Order of Saint Clare, the Third Order of Saint Francis and the Custody of the Holy Land.

Attila the Hun (flourished *c.* 406–453)

Ruler of the Huns from 434 until his death. He was known as 'the scourge of God' from his incessant and largely merciless depredations on the Roman Empire.

Augustine (354–430)

Augustine of Hippo was an early Christian theologian from North Africa. He was one of the most prolific Latin writers. The theology of Augustine had a great influence on Martin Luther and other Reformers.

Benedict XI (1240–1304)

Born as Nicola di Boccassio, and also known as Niccolò of Treviso. He succeeded Boniface VIII as pope in 1303 and died eight months later. He was succeeded by Clement V.

Benedict XIII (1328–1423)

A Spanish nobleman and teacher of canon law, born as Pedro Martínez de Luna y Pérez de Gotor. He was elected as the second Avignon antipope in 1394. In 1398, the Kingdom of France withdrew its recognition of the Avignon papacy. Most of his cardinals abandoned him and only five remaining faithful to him. Despite this, Benedict clung to power. Some of his supporters moved to Scotland. In 1413, he issued a series of papal bulls, which led to the establishment of the University of St Andrews. The university's coat of arms continues to include a depiction of Benedict. The Council of Pisa (1409) declared him a schismatic and deposed both him and the 'official' Roman pope, Gregory XII. Neither man acquiesced, and the Council proceeded to elect a third competing pope, the Pisan antipope Alexander V. After Benedict died, he was succeeded by the Avignon antipope Clement VIII.

Böhler, Peter (1712–1775)
A German-English Moravian missionary and bishop, undertook missionary work in America. Before going there, he led a Bible study in Fetter Lane, London, and had a great influence on John Wesley.

Boniface VIII (1230–1303)
Pope from 1294 to 1303. He was involved in prolonged conflict with Philip IV of France, who wished to raise funds by taxing the Roman Catholic Church.

Bracciolini, Poggio (1380–1459)
Gian Francesco Poggio Bracciolini was an Italian scholar and an early Renaissance humanist. He was responsible for rediscovering and recovering a great number of classical Latin manuscripts, which were mostly decaying and forgotten in German, Swiss, and French monastic libraries. He wrote eloquently about Jerome when he appeared before the Council of Constance.

di Brescia, Arnaldo [Arnold of Brescia] (*c.* 1090–1155)

An Augustinian, who became prior of an abbey in Brescia in Lombardy, northern Italy. He boldly opposed the pope's claims to universal supremacy. He also declared that, in order that the world should live in peace, the Church must return to the purity and simplicity of apostolic times. Because of his views, he was exiled at least three times and was eventually arrested. Arnold was hanged by the papacy, then was burned posthumously and his ashes were thrown into the River Tiber.

z Brodu, Michal

Pronounced Michal Zbrodoo. See **de Causis, Michal**.

Bruni, Leonardo (1370–1444)

An Italian humanist and historian, who is held to be the most important humanist historian of the early Renaissance.

von Bucka, Johann (died 1430)

Pronounced Yohann von Bootska. Also known as John the Iron, he was Bishop of Litomyšl (pronounced Leetomeeshl) from 1392 to 1418. He was an opponent of Hus and travelled with Štěpán z Pálče to the Council of Constance. Von Bucka collected donations to pay the expenses of people who wished to make a deposition against Hus under oath. Litomyšl is a town in Bohemia, 85 miles (136 km) east of Prague.

Calvin, Jean [John Calvin] (1509–1564)

French Reformer.

Cambrai, Cardinal of

See **Ailly, Pierre d'**.

de Causis, Michal [Michael of Deutschbrod] (before 1380–*c.* 1432)

The common cognomen for Michal z Brodu. He was born in Deutschbrod (now known as Havlíčkův Brod, pronounced Havlee<u>tsh</u>koov Brot), a town 61 miles (97 km) southeast of Prague. He was a German-speaking parish priest of St Adalbertus in Prague. Václav entrusted him with money to repair silver mines but he absconded with the money and went to Rome. Later he was appointed as a prosecutor or 'Advocate in matters of faith' (Latin: *procurator de causis fidei*) by the Pisan antipope John XXIII and was therefore generally known by the nickname Michal de Causis. He was the agent of the Prague clergy at the Curia (papal Court) and prepared the accusation against Hus in 1411, which led to the second decree of excommunication against Hus. Along with Štěpán z Pálče, Michal de Causis led the trial against Hus at the Council of Constance.

Charles V (1500–1558)

Ruler of the Spanish Empire from 1516 and of the Holy Roman Empire from 1521. He summoned Martin Luther to the Imperial Diet of Worms in 1521, promising him safe conduct. Shortly after Luther left Worms, he outlawed Luther and his followers.

z Chlumu, Jan [John of Chlum, or John Kepka of Chlum] (died 1425)

Pronounced Yan Z<u>ch</u>loomoo. One of three noblemen who escorted Hus to Constance. He staunchly defended Hus and sought his release from captivity. Many Czech towns and villages are called Chlum. In the case of Jan z Chlumu, he hailed from Chlum in the north of Bohemia, 55 miles (88 km) north of Prague.

Clement V (c. 1264–1314)

Born as Raymond Bertrand de Got. He was pope from 1305 to 1314. Clement moved the papal court from Rome to Avignon, ushering in the period known as the Avignon Papacy.

Clement VII (1342–1394)

Born as Robert de Genève. He was elected to the papacy by the French cardinals who opposed Urban VI, and became the first antipope to reside in Avignon.

Clement of Alexandria (c. 150–c. 215)

A theologian who taught in Alexandria, Egypt.

Constantine, Emperor (c. 272–337)

Roman Emperor from 306 to 337 AD. He played an influential role in the proclamation of the Edict of Milan in 313, which decreed tolerance for Christianity in the Roman Empire. He called the First Council of Nicaea in 325 AD, at which the Church adopted the Nicene Creed. The Donation of Constantine is a forged decree by which Constantine supposedly transferred authority over Rome and the western part of the Roman Empire to the Pope. The decree was probably composed in the 8th century and it was used in support of claims of political authority by the papacy.

Cossa, Baldassare
See John XIII.

Cyril (826–869)

Born in Thessalonica, in present-day Greece. In 862, Prince Rastislav (pronounced Rastislaf) of Great Moravia ejected missionaries of the Roman Catholic Church from his territories and requested that Byzantine missionaries should be sent to evangelise his Slavic subjects. Cyril and his brother, Methodius, undertook this work, along with assistants whom they trained. In addition, the brothers translated portions of the Bible into a language known as Old Church Slavonic.

Dacher, Eberhard (dates unknown)

He attended the Council of Constance and was the author of *Konstanzer Chronik* [*Chronicle of Constance*], which contains his contemporaneous account of the Council of Constance.

Dante (*c.* 1265–1321)

The commonly used name for Durante degli Alighieri, a pre-eminent Italian poet. He wrote in criticism of the alleged 'Donation of Constantine' in his work, *Divina Commedia* [*The Divine Comedy*].

David, Christian (dates unknown)

A tutor to the Baron von Schweinitz, and later a Moravian missionary. After a meeting with Zinzendorf, the latter established a community for refugees belonging to the Unity of the Brethren, who had fled Counter-Reformation persecution in Moravia and settled in Germany from 1772.

z Dubé, Václav [Wenceslaus of Dubá] (dates unknown)

Pronounced Vatslaf Zdoobeh. A Bohemian nobleman who accompanied Hus to the Council of Constance. Dubá is a town in Bohemia situated 32 miles (51 km) north of Prague.

Eugene IV (1383–1447)

Born in Venice as Gabriele Condulmer. He was elected pope in 1431 as the successor of Martin V. At the Diet of Nürnberg that year, he preached the fifth and final crusade against the Hussites.

185

Ferdinand I of Austria (1503–1564)

A Spanish prince, who was the grandson of Emperor Maximilian I. He became King of Bohemia and Hungary from 1526, and Holy Roman Emperor from 1558. In 1547, he and his son Maximilian participated in the victorious campaign of Emperor Charles V against the German Protestants. That year, he also defeated a Protestant revolt in Bohemia, which allowed him to increase his power base. Ferdinand also sought to strengthen the position of the Roman Catholic Church in the Bohemian lands, and favoured the deployment of the Jesuits there.

Ferdinand II Štýrský [Ferdinand II of Styria] (1578–1637)

Pronounced Ferdinand Shteerskee. Holy Roman Emperor from 1617. His aim was to restore Catholicism as the only religion in the Empire, and to suppress Protestantism. His actions brought about the Thirty Years' War. Styria is a province in the southeast of present-day Austria.

Florence, Cardinal of
See **Zabarella, Francesco**.

Friedrich I von Brandenburg [Frederick of Brandenburg] (1371–1440)

One of the Imperial Electors. He led the third and fourth Roman Catholic crusades against the Hussites.

Friedrich IV [Frederick IV] (1382–1439)

Duke of Austria from 1402 until his death in 1439. He sided with the Pisan antipope John XXIII, whom he helped on his flight from the Council of Constance in March 1415. As a result, Friedrich was placed under an imperial ban but succeeded in retaining some of his lands.

Friedrich V [Frederick V] (1596–1632)

Elector Palatine of the Rhine from 1610 to 1623. He married Elizabeth Stuart in 1613 and served as King of Bohemia from 1619 to 1620. He was forced to abdicate after the Battle of Bílá Hora [White Mountain]. The brevity of his reign earned him the derisive nickname of 'the Winter King'.

de Got, Bertrand, Archbishop of Bordeaux
See **Clement V**

Gregory XI (*c.* 1329–1370)

The seventh and last of the Avignon popes. He returned the papal Court to Rome, ending the Avignon papacy. The Western Schism followed shortly after his death.

Gregory XII (*c.* 1326–1417)

Roman pope from 1406 to 1415. He reigned at the same time as the rival Avignon antipope Benedict XIII. Gregory had the support of Archbishop Zbyněk of Prague and the German branch of Prague University. At the Council of Constance, Gregory was forced to resign in order to end the Western Schism. The papacy remained vacant until Gregory's death, when Martin V was appointed.

Guzmán, Dominic (1170–1221)

A Castilian priest who was noted for his attempts to bring the heretic Albigensians back to the fold of the Roman Catholic Church. Later he became the founder of the Dominican Order, a preaching monastic order. In 1234, he was canonised (made a Roman Catholic 'saint') by Pope Gregory IX.

Habsburský, Matyáš [Matthias of Habsburg] (1557–1619)

Pronounced Matias Habsburský. Son of the Holy Roman Emperor, Maximilian II. In turn, Matyáš became king of Bohemia in 1611 and emperor the following year. He implemented some conciliatory policies towards Protestants.

Heinrich VII [Henry VII] of Luxembourg (*c.* 1275–1313)

The King of Germany from 1308 and Holy Roman Emperor from 1312. He was the first emperor of the House of Luxembourg. His son married a sister of the last Slav king of Bohemia and then ruled Bohemia as Jan Lucemburský [John of Luxembourg] from 1310 until 1346.

Heluvel, John (dates unknown)

A priest who conversed with Hus in Nürnberg, during Hus's journey to the Council of Constance.

Henry of Winchester (*c.* 1375–1447)

Henry Beaufort was a half-brother of Henry IV of England. He was Lord Chancellor of England, and became Bishop of Winchester in 1404. Pope Martin V appointed Henry as a cardinal in 1426, and made him a Papal Legate the following year. He led the fourth papal crusade against the Hussites but his forces were routed in the Battle of Tachov (pronounced Tachof) in 1427.

von Hochheim, Eckhart (*c.* 1260–*c.* 1328)

A German theologian, philosopher and mystic, also known as Meister [Master] Eckhart. Towards the end of his life, he was tried as a heretic by Pope John XXII. It seems that he died before the verdict was delivered.

Hübner, John (dates unknown)
A German theologian in Prague. He petitioned the pope about forty-five of Wycliffe's propositions as well as about the philosophical teaching on Realism which predominated at the university. Twenty-four of the propositions had been condemned in England in 1382, and the remainder were compiled by Hübner,

Hus, Jan [John Huss] (c. 1369–1415)
Pronounced Yan Hooss.

Innocent VII (1339–1406)
Roman pope from 1404 until his death in 1406. The rival Avignon antipope Benedict XIII reigned during this period. He ordered Archbishop Zbyněk to take measures to destroy Wycliffe's teaching in Bohemia.

z Janova, Matěj [Matthew of Janow] (died 1394)
Pronounced Mattyey Zyanova. He was born in the town of Mladá Vožice (pronounced Mlada Vozhitseh), 41 miles (66 km) south of Prague. He was canon of Prague Cathedral from 1381 until his death. Matěj z Janova was an influential writer, and his book *De Regulis Veteris et Novi Testamentis* [*The Principles of the Old and New Testament*] helped to prepare the way for Hus' reformation. Matěj z Janova advocated daily communion, and he strove to remove the images of 'saints' and their relics from churches, because of the abuses he witnessed arising from their veneration. After the Synod of Prague (1389) prohibited daily communion and defended the veneration of images, Matěj retracted his views and swore repeatedly that he had unfailing loyalty towards the Catholic Church, and in this way he escaped punishment.

z Jesenice, Jan [John of Jessinic] (died *c.* 1420)

Pronounced Yan Zyeseneetseh. He was both a friend of Hus and his lawyer. He represented Hus before a papal court in 1410, but during the trial he was forbidden to act on Hus's behalf. Later he was imprisoned in Rome but escaped to Bologna, where he was recaptured and once more imprisoned. He then returned to Bohemia. Jan z Jesenice represented Hus at the Council of Constance. He became the head of the Calixtines after Hus's death. Jesenice lies on the southern border of the present city of Prague.

Jerome of Prague (1379–1416)

In Czech, Jeroným Pražský (pronounced Yeroneem Pra<u>zh</u>skee). He is often called Hieronymus from the Latin form of his first name. A Bohemian scholastic theologian and reformer. He became acquainted with Wycliffe's writings when he studied at Oxford University. Jerome was one of the chief followers of Jan Hus and eloquently protested against the sale of indulgences. At the Council of Constance, he recanted but later repented of this action and was burned for 'heresy'.

John XXIII (*c.* 1370–1419)

Baldassare Cossa was a notoriously licentious cardinal who helped to convene the Council of Pisa in 1409. The Council appointed Alexander V as pope (rivalling the Roman pope Gregory XII and the Avignon antipope Benedict XIII) but he died a year later. Cossa was then appointed as his successor, taking the name John XXIII, and he reigned from 1410 until the Council of Constance in 1415. At the time of his appointment in 1410, his main enemy was King Ladislaus of Naples. John issued a bull of excommunication against Ladislaus, and ordered a crusade to be preached against him. In order to fund this, John authorised Vacláv Tiem to sell indulgences in Bohemia. During the Council of Constance, it was resolved that all three rival popes should abdicate. John XIII fled from Constance and was deposed by the Council in 1415. He was later tried for heresy, simony, schism and immorality, and found guilty on all counts.

John Scotus Erigena (or Eriugena) (*c.* 815–*c.* 877)
An Irish theologian and philosopher.

Karel IV [Charles IV] (1316–1378)
He succeeded to the throne of Bohemia in 1347, and was the first Bohemian king to become Holy Roman Emperor (1355). The 'Golden Age' of Bohemia occurred under his reign.

Komenský, Jan Amos [John Amos Comenius] (1592–1670)
Pronounced Yan Ahmoss Komenskee. A theologian, philosopher and internationally acclaimed educationalist from Moravia. He served as the last bishop of Unity of the Brethren and led the Brethren into exile in Poland when the Habsburg Counter-Reformation persecuted the Protestants in Bohemia. He was one of the early champions of universal education, a concept eventually propounded in his book *Didactica Magna* [*The Great Didactic*].

Korybutovič, Zikmund [Sigismund Korybut] (*c.* 1395–1435)
Pronounced Zikmoont Korybutovitsh. He was the son of the Grand Duke of Lithuania and was raised in Poland. Zikmund was his father's regent for Bohemia. He became a military commander of the Hussite army, and a governor of Bohemia and Prague during the Hussite Wars.

Kříž (dates unknown)
Pronounced K<u>rzhee</u>zh. A Prague merchant who helped to
found Bethlehem Chapel.

**Lacembok z Chlumu, Jindřich [Henry Latzenbock of
Chlum] (dates unknown)**
Pronounced Yeend<u>rzhee</u>ch Latsembock Z<u>chl</u>oomoo. One of
three nobles who escorted Hus to the Council of Constance.
Unlike the other two escorts, he repudiated Hus's doctrines and
approved of his condemnation. Chlum is a town in the north of
Bohemia, 55 miles (88 km) north of Prague.

Ladislaus of Naples (1377–1414)
A licentious king of Naples, who was a skilled political and military leader. He was a staunch supporter of the Roman popes
Innocent VII and Gregory XII. The Pisan antipope John XXIII
was a bitter enemy of Ladislaus, and commanded the sale of
indulgences to raise money to fight Ladislaus.

**z Litomyšle, Mikuláš [Nicholas of Litomyšl] (c. 1350–
c. 1404)**
Pronounced Meekulash Zleetomeeshleh. One of Hus's teachers
at the University of Prague. He enthusiastically embraced the
teachings of Wycliffe and supported Hus when Hus came under
attack for his lectures at the University of Prague. Litomyšl is a
town in Bohemia, 85 miles (136 km) east of Prague.

Lodi, Arrigoni of (died 1435)
An Italian bishop who preached at the Council of Constance,
immediately before the formal condemnation of Hus.

Lucemburská, Anna [Anne of Bohemia] (1366–1394)

Pronounced Anna Lootsemboorska. She was the eldest daughter of Karel IV and was the sister of the future Václav IV. She married Richard II of England in Westminster Abbey in 1382, and died childless twelve years later. She favoured Wycliffe and encouraged him in the translation of the Bible into English.

Lucemburský, Jan [John of Luxembourg or John of Bohemia] (1296–1346)

Pronounced Yan Lootsemboorskee. A son of Heinrich VII of Luxembourg. He married a sister of the last Slav king of Bohemia and then ruled Bohemia as Jan Lucemburský from 1310 until 1346. He became blind around the age of forty and was then known as John the Blind. He died in the French-led forces fighting the English in the Battle of Crécy in northern France.

Lucemburský, Zikmund [Sigismund of Luxembourg] (1368–1437)

Pronounced Zikmoont Lootsemboorskee. He was the younger half-brother of Václav IV. Among many titles, he was King of Bohemia from 1419 and Holy Roman Emperor for four years from 1433 until 1437. Zikmund was the last male member of the House of Luxembourg.

Ludvík Jagellonský [Louis II of Hungary, or Louis the Jagiellonian] (1506–1526)

Pronounced Loodveek Yagellonsky. The Jagiellonian royal dynasty was founded by Jogaila, the Grand Duke of Lithuania, who in 1386 was baptized as Władysław (pronounced Vwadyswaf), married Queen regnant Jadwiga (pronounced Yadveega) of Poland, and was crowned King of Poland as Władysław II Jagiełło (pronounced Yagyewwoh). The dynasty reigned in several countries between the 14th and 16th centuries. At various times, members of the dynasty were Kings of Poland, Grand Dukes of Lithuania, Kings of Hungary, and Kings of Bohemia. After the death of his father, King Vladislav Jagellonský [Vladislaus II], in 1516, Ludvík became king of Bohemia and Hungary at the age of ten. He died ten years later in a battle with forces of the Ottoman Empire, which destroyed most of the Hungarian army.

Ludwig III [Louis III] (1378–1436)

Ludwig was the Elector Palatine and acted as vicar for Sigismund, Holy Roman Emperor. He was the emperor's bearer during the Council of Constance and in this capacity he executed the sentences against Jan Hus and Jerome of Prague. He also arrested the antipope John XXIII in 1415.

Luther, Martin (1483–1546)

German Reformer.

Martin V (1369–1431)

The Council of Constance deposed the Pisan antipope John XXIII in 1415 but remained divided by the conflicting claims of Gregory XII and the Avignon antipope Benedict XIII. The election of Martin V as pope in 1417 effectively ended the Western Schism. He issued a papal Bull in 1420, inviting all Christendom to participate in the first Roman Catholic anti-Hussite crusade. The aim was to destroy the Wycliffites, the Hussites, and all other 'heretics' in Bohemia, promising full indulgences to all those who would either take part themselves or would pay for a substitute.

Maximilian II (1527–1576)

King of Bohemia from 1562. He succeeded his father, Ferdinand I of Austria, as ruler of the Holy Roman Empire in 1564.

He tolerated Protestants and granted freedom of worship to the Protestant nobility. Spanish opposition prevented his plans for reform in the Roman Catholic Church, which included granting priests the right to marry.

Methodius (815–885)

Born in Thessalonica, in present-day Greece. In 862, Prince Rastislav of Great Moravia ejected missionaries of the Roman Catholic Church from his territories and requested that Byzantine missionaries should be sent to evangelise his Slavic subjects. Methodius and his brother, Cyril, undertook this work, along with assistants whom they trained. In addition, the brothers translated portions of the Bible into a language known as Old Church Slavonic.

Milíč z Kroměříže, Jan [Jan Milíč of Kroměříž] (died 1374)

Pronounced Yan Meeleetsh Zkromyerzheezhe. He became a priest in 1350. After that, he was a long-time employee of the Court of Karel IV, eventually becoming the king's secretary. In 1363, he resigned from his posts so that he could be a full-time priest. He preached to scholars in Latin and to the laity in Bohemian, which was a novelty. He witnessed against the riches of the mendicant friars, and helped to recover prostitutes in Prague. Through studying the Scriptures, he became convinced that the 'abomination of desolation' was now seen in the Roman Catholic Church, and that antichrist had come. In 1367, he went to Rome to expound these views. He was thrown into prison by the Inquisition, but was freed by the pope, Urban V. Prior to Hus, he was the most influential preacher of the emerging Bohemian Reformation. Kroměříž is a town in Moravia, located 143 miles (230 km) southeast of Prague.

z Mladoňovic, Petr [Peter of Mladoňovice] (1390–1451)

Pronounced Petr Zmladonyovits. A scribe who was a follower of Hus. He chronicled the trial, condemnation and martyrdom of Hus in Constance. He returned to Bohemia and was associated with the Utraquist faction at the University. He was expelled from Prague in 1427 and spent the rest of his days on the estate of a Calixtine nobleman. Mladoňovice (pronounced Mladonyovitseh) is a village in southern Bohemia, near the border with Austria, situated 91 miles (147 km) from Prague.

z Mühlheimu, Hanušem [John of Mülheim or Milheim] (dates unknown)

Pronounced Hanooshem Zmulheimoo. He was a member of a patrician family, which originated from Silesia in present-day Poland. He was a member of the royal Court in Prague, and participated in various diplomatic missions. Hanušem z Mühlheimu was one of the founders of Bethlehem Chapel in 1391.

Nazareth, Nicholas of (dates unknown)

Papal inquisitor in Bohemia around the time of the Council of Constance.

Otakar I [Ottokar I] (c. 1155–1230)

Pronounced as written. King of Bohemia from 1198. German immigration to Bohemia began under his reign.

Otakar II [Ottokar II] (1233–1278)

Pronounced as written. King of Bohemia from 1253. He established many new cities and expanded the Bohemian territories. He is considered one of the most successful Bohemian rulers, and the country became notably wealthy during his reign.

Otto III von Hachberg (1388–1451)

Bishop of Constance from 1410 to 1434, and host of the Council of Constance. He was the eldest son of Margrave Rudolf III of Hachberg-Sausenberg. Although he was the second person named Otto in the Hachberg-Sausenberg family, he is consistently called Otto III because he was the third bishop of Constance named Otto.

z Pálče, Štěpán [Stephen Paletz] (*c.* 1370–1423)

Pronounced Shtyepan Spaltsheh. A priest who became rector of Prague University in 1400. He was a great advocate of Wycliffe's teachings. In 1408, Stanislav ze Znojma and Štěpán attended the Council of Pisa, but both were captured and imprisoned for some time. Like Hus, he was an opponent of indulgences. Later Štěpán began gradually to deviate from Wycliffe's teachings and ended up attacking them. King Václav banished him from Bohemia when he refused to attend meetings aimed at restoring peace to Bohemia. Štěpán was one of the most implacable enemies of Hus at the Council of Constance, describing him as 'the worst heretic'.

z Pardubic, Arnošt [Ernest of Pardubice] (1297–1364)

Pronounced Arnosht Spardoobeets. A Bohemian nobleman who was appointed as the first Archbishop of Prague in 1344. He was also an advisor and diplomat to Emperor Karel IV. Pardubice is a town in Bohemia, 60 miles (96 km) east of Prague.

Petrarch (1304–1374)

The anglicised name of Francesco Petrarco, an Italian scholar, poet and Roman Catholic Church diplomat. He was one of the first Renaissance humanists. In the courses of his travels, he collected fragile old Latin manuscripts and was a prime mover in the recovery of knowledge from writers of Rome and Greece.

Philippe IV [Philip IV of France] (1268–1314)

King of France from 1285 until his death. Pope Boniface VIII condemned him for his spendthrift lifestyle. Philippe imposed heavy taxes on the French clergy, which caused uproar within the Roman Catholic Church and the papacy, and a prolonged diplomatic battle ensued. After Boniface died, the French archbishop Bertrand de Got was elected pope as Clement V and the official seat of the papacy was moved to Avignon at Philippe's instigation.

Pius II (1405–1464)

Born as Enea Silvio Bartolomeo Piccolomini, also known as Æneas Sylvius Bartholomeus. He was elected pope as Pius II in 1458 and reigned until his death in 1464.

z Poděbrad, Jiří [George of Poděbrady] (1420-1471)

Pronounced Yeerzhee Spodyebrat. His father was one of the leaders of the Utraquists. At the age of fourteen, Jiří took part in the Battle of Lipany (1434), which marked the downfall of the Taborites. He later became leader of the Hussites. Jiří was King of Bohemia from 1458 to 1471 and he attempted to rule in a moderate manner. All Jiří's attempts to establish peace with Rome proved ineffectual and he made enemies among the nobles of the papal party, who formed an alliance against him. In 1466, Pope Paul II excommunicated Jiří and pronounced his deposition as king of Bohemia, releasing all subjects of the Bohemian crown from their oaths of allegiance to Jiří. The Bohemian town of Poděbrady is located on the river Labe, 31 miles (50 km) east of Prague.

Přemyslovna, Eliška [Elizabeth of Bohemia] (1292–1330)

Pronounced Elishka P<u>rzh</u>emyslovna. The first wife of Jan Lucemburský, and mother of Karel IV.

Prokop Holý [Prokop the Great] (*c.* 1380–1434)

Pronounced Prokop Holee. Initially Prokop was an Utraquist priest. Later he became a Taborite and a Hussite general, and was notably victorious in battles against the Roman Catholic anti-Hussite crusades. Prokop was the leading member of the Hussite delegation to the Council of Basel. Following prolonged strife between the moderate and strict factions of the Hussites, he and his brother, Prokop Malý, perished in the battle of Lipany.

Prokop Malý [Prokop the Lesser] (died 1434)

Pronounced Prokop Malee. The younger brother of Prokop Holý. He joined Žižka's army at a young age, and officiated at Žižka's funeral in 1424. He then became a leader of the Taborite forces. Prokop accompanied his brother, Prokop Holý, in the Hussite delegation to the Council of Basel. Following prolonged strife between the moderate and strict factions of the Hussites, both brothers perished in the battle of Lipany.

Richard II of England (1367–1400)

He succeeded to the throne of England when he was aged ten, and reigned from 1377 until he was deposed in 1399. In 1382, he married Anna Lucemburská [Anne of Bohemia], sister of King Václav IV [Wenceslas IV]. The marriage was not popular in England. Anna died of the plague in 1394, and in 1396 Richard married the seven year-old Isabella of Valois (1389–1409) in an arranged marriage, by which she became Queen Consort of England.

de la Rochetaillée, Jean (died 1437)

The titular Roman Catholic Patriarch of Constantinople from 1412 to 1423.

Rokycana, Jan [John of Rokycany] (*c.* 1396–1471)

Pronounced Yan Rockytsana. An Augustinian monk in his young days. He left the monastery to study at Prague University, where he graduated in 1415. He became a Calixtine and opposed the radical Taborites under Žižka. He brokered peace between the warring Hussite factions in 1424, and later became Utraquist bishop of Prague.

Rudolf II [Rudolph II] (1552–1612)

Pronounced as written. He became king of Bohemia in 1575, and the following year he became Holy Roman Emperor. Rudolf was tolerant of Protestantism and other religions including Judaism, despite his upbringing at his uncle's Roman Catholic court in Spain. He ratified the free exercise of religion that the Moravians had received under Maximilian II, and allowed them to erect churches.

Ruprecht von der Pfalz [Rupert of the Palatinate, or Rupert, Count Palatine] (1352–1410)

Ruprecht was the Elector Palatine from 1398 and King of the Germans from 1400. He was the unsuccessful rival of King Václav IV as candidate for the crown of the Holy Roman Empire.

van Ruusbroec, Jan [John of Ruysbroeck] (1293/1294–1381)

He was named after his native village of Ruusbroec (present-day Ruisbroek) in Flanders, on the outskirts of Brussels. Jan became a priest in Brussels where he became known as a writer against the Beghards. He became one of the influential Flemish mystics and wrote in Flemish (Dutch) in order to get a wide readership.

Seuse, Heinrich [Henry Suso] (*c.* 1295–1366)
He was born Heinrich von Berg, but later took his mother's name as a mark of honour to her. He entered the Dominican Order in Constance at the age of thirteen. Five years later, he underwent a religious experience, which may have been conversion. He later went to Strasbourg, and then to Cologne. In the latter city, he encountered Meister Eckhart and possibly also Johannes Tauler, two noted German mystics.

Siena, Catherine of (1347–1380)
An Italian scholastic theologian, who had miraculous 'visions'. She worked to bring the papacy of Gregory XI back to Rome from Avignon.

Spangenberg, August (1704–1792)
A German theologian and a bishop of the Moravian Brethren. As successor of Count Nicolaus Ludwig Zinzendorf, he helped develop international missions, as well as defining the theology and organisation of the German Moravian Church. John Wesley met him in Georgia, USA.

St Angelo, Peter (dates unknown)
A cardinal who was sent by the Pisan antipope John XIII to Prague, to enforce the second excommunication of Hus in 1411.

von Staupitz, Johann von (*c.* 1460–1524)
He was 'Vicar General' of the Augustinian Order in Germany and was dean of the theological faculty in the University of Wittenberg. When Luther was a monk in the Augustinian monastery in Erfurt, he felt compelled to confess his sins in detail to

von Staupitz. In reply, von Staupitz counselled him on the means of grace and on salvation through the sacrificial death of Christ. After the Diet of Worms in 1518, Luther was declared a heretic. As head of the Augustinians, von Staupitz was appointed to plead with Luther on the question of indulgences. In 1520, Pope Leo X demanded an abjuration and revocation of heresy from von Staupitz. He refused to revoke, on the grounds that he had never asserted Luther's 'heresies', but he did abjure and recognised the authority of the Pope as his judge. Subsequently, in 1522, von Staupitz became a monk in Salzburg and died as an abbot there.

z Štěkně, Jan (dates unknown)

Pronounced Yan Zshtyeknyeh. A famous preacher in Prague, who became a teacher of Hus.

ze Stříbra, Jakoubek [Jacob of Stříbro or of Mies] (1372–1429)

Pronounced Yakowbek Zestrzheebra. An outspoken supporter of Hus. In 1410, he took part in the public debates regarding Wycliffe, and defended the Englishman against Archbishop Zbyněk's condemnation. Jakoubek's study of Scripture and the Church Fathers led him to believe that withholding the communion chalice from the laity was an unscriptural practice of the Roman Catholic Church. He administered the chalice to his parishioners, in spite of opposition, and his example was quickly followed by other priests in Prague. Stříbro [Mies in German] is situated in the west of Bohemia, near the current border with Germany, 68 miles (109 km) southwest of Prague.

Stuart, Elizabeth (1596–1662)

Born at Falkland Palace, Fife, to James VI of Scotland and his wife, Anne of Denmark. She married Friedrich V at the Palace of Whitehall in 1613. Friedrich became king of Bohemia in November 1619. Her reign ended when Friedrich abdicated after his defeat by Ferdinand at the Battle of Bílá Hora [White Mountain] on 8th November 1620]. Due to the brevity of her reign, Elizabeth is known by the derisive nickname of 'the Winter Queen'.

Tauler, Johannes (c. 1300–1361)

He was a German Dominican monk. Tauler came from Strasbourg and was educated there. He was influenced by the teaching of Meister Eckhart, who was also in Strasbourg, but it is not clear what relationship existed between them. Tauler began preaching around 1300 and became famous as a mystic.

Tertullian (c. 155–c. 240)

An early Christian theologian from North Africa.

Tiem, Vacláv [Wenceslaus Tiem] (dates unknown)

Pronounced Vatslaf Teem. Tiem was Dean of Passau in Austria, and subsequently became the papal legate in Bohemia. He sold indulgences on behalf of antipope John XIII in order to raise money for the antipope to fight against Ladislaus of Naples. Hus and Jerome of Prague preached against the trade.

z Uničova, Albík [Albert of Uničov] (c. 1358–1427)

Pronounced Albeek Zoonitshova. A physician and lawyer, who was personal physician to Vacláv IV from 1399. He was briefly Archbishop of Prague, from 1411 to 1412. During the Hussite Wars, Albík fled the country and left most of his possessions in

Prague. Uničov (pronounced Ooneetshoff) is a town in Moravia, located 122 miles (197 km) east of Prague.

Urban V (1310–1370)

He was pope in Avignon from 1362 until his death. Urban pressed for reform throughout his pontificate and he also oversaw the restoration and construction of churches and monasteries. Milíč appealed against his accusers to Urban, but when he went to the papal court, he was imprisoned.

Urban VI (1318–1389)

He was pope from 1378. Urban appointed Matěj z Janova to the post of Canon of the Cathedral Church of Prague. The Western Schism began during his reign.

Václav III [Wenceslaus III] (1289–1306)

Pronounced Vatslaf. Václav was King of Hungary from 1301 to 1305, and King of Bohemia and Poland from 1305. He was murdered by an unknown assassin and, as he had no male issue, he was the last Slav king of Bohemia.

Václav IV [Wenceslaus IV] (1361–1419)

Pronounced Vatslaf. He was born in Nürnberg, the son of Emperor Charles IV. Charles had him crowned King of Bohemia at the age of two year in 1363, and ten years later, in 1373, he obtained for Václav the position of Elector of Brandenburg. In 1376, Charles asserted the election of Václav as King of the Romans. When Charles died in 1378, Václav inherited the Crown of Bohemia and became the Emperor-elect of the Holy Roman Empire. However, due to internal strife in Bohemia, he did not seek a coronation ceremony and eventually his younger half-brother, Zikmund Lucemburský (King of Hungary), became Emperor. As Bohemian king, Václav sought to protect

Hus and his followers from the demands of the Roman Catholic Church for their suppression as 'heretics'. He provided an escort for Hus and his companions to travel to the Council of Constance, but was powerless to prevent the condemnation and execution of Hus.

z Vechty, Konrád (c. 1364–1431)

Pronounced Konrat Sfechtee. Konrád was born in Vechta, which was then in the German state of Westphalia but is now situated in Lower Saxony. He was a capable financier who came to serve in the Court of Václav IV. Konrád eventually became Archbishop of Prague from 1413 to 1421. He took the side of the Hussites during the Hussite Wars, despite remaining a Catholic prelate, and was deposed as archbishop by the papal Curia.

Vladislav Jagellonský [Vladislaus II of Hungary] (1456–1516)

Pronounced Vladislaf Yagellonskee. He was King of Bohemia from 1471 to 1516, and King of Hungary and Croatia from 1490 to 1516. He was specifically required to acknowledge the existence of two 'nations' (the Catholic and Hussite Estates) in his realm in accordance with the *Compactata* of Basel, although the Pope had already condemned the compacts in 1462. His reign was beset by problems in both realms, with the result that the nobility widely extended their powers and strengthened their hold over an already oppressed peasantry.

Waldhauser, Konrád [Conrad of Waldhausen] (c. 1326–1369)

An Austrian priest who arrived in Prague in 1363 at the invitation of Karel IV. He preached against the corruption of the priests and was popular with the citizens. His preaching led against pride and licentious behaviour led many of them to forsake worldly behaviour. He is regarded as a forerunner of Hus.

Waldo, Peter (*c.* 1140–*c.* 1205)
A Frenchman from Lyon, the reputed founder of the Waldensians.

Wesley, John (1703–1791)
Ordained in the Church of England in 1726. After an unsuccessful ministry in Georgia, America, he returned to England and came under the influence of a religious meeting of Moravians, led by Peter Böhler. Along with his brother Charles, and George Whitefield, John Wesley founded the Methodist Church. Like the Moravians, Wesley's theology was Arminian, in contrast to Whitefield's Calvinism.

Wycliffe, John (*c.* mid-1320s–1384)
He was an influential dissident within the Roman Catholic priesthood during the 14th century. He attacked the privileged status of the clergy and the luxury and pomp of local parishes and their ceremonies. Wycliffe issued a translation directly from the Latin Vulgate into Middle English from about 1382 to 1395. Wycliffe's followers were known as Lollards and followed his lead in advocating biblical doctrines and practices and attacking Romanism. Historians have regarded the Lollard movement as the precursor to the Protestant Reformation. Wycliffe's writings in Latin greatly influenced the philosophy and teaching of Hus.

Zabarella, Francesco (1360–1417)
Cardinal of Florence. He was the youngest cardinal at the Council of Constance. Zabarella attempted to get Hus and Jerome to sign abjurations.

Zajíc z Hazmburka, Zbyněk [Zbyněk Zajíc of Hasenburg] (c. 1376–1411)

Pronounced Zbeenyek Zahyeets Z-hazmburka). An illiterate Bohemian nobleman, who was a military adviser to King Vacláv IV. He had no previous position in the church when became the Archbishop of Prague in 1403 in consequence of his noble background. Initially Archbishop Zbyněk was sympathetic to Hus and protected him, but later he strongly opposed his views and his attempts to reform the Roman Catholic Church. Under pressure from antipope Alexander V and the clergy of Prague in 1409, Zbyněk ordered the books of Wycliffe and others to be condemned and burned, and he proclaimed a ban against Hus.

von Zinzendorf, Count Nikolaus Ludwig (1700–1760)

Nikolaus Ludwig, Reichsgraf [Imperial Count] von Zinzendorf und Pottendorf was a German Lutheran of the pietist movement. He provided shelter for the German-speaking Moravian exiles at Herrnhut. He became a bishop of the Moravian Church and founder of the Herrnhuter Brüdergemeinde [the Herrnhut Brethren Congregation].

Žižka z Trocnova, Jan [John Žižka of Trocnov] (1360–1424)

Pronounced Yan Zheeshka Strotsnova. Bohemian general and leader of the radical Hussite Taborite faction. He is considered to be among the greatest military leaders and innovators of all time. He used unorthodox methods, such as armoured wagons, which provided safe mobile platforms for troops with firearms. Žižka exercised strict military discipline. He is one of several military commanders in history who never lost a battle. He was blinded in one eye early in his career, and in 1421 he was severely wounded during the siege of a castle, losing the use of his remaining eye. Despite being totally blind, he continued to successfully command the armies of the Taborites for the remainder of his life. Internal dissent among the Hussites led to civil war in 1423. Žižka, as leader of the Taborites, defeated the men of Prague and the Utraquist nobles. Jan Rokycana helped to bring about peace between the warring factions. When Žižka died, his Taborite followers named themselves Orphans because they felt they had lost their father.

ze Znojma, Petr [Peter of Znojmo or of Znaim] (dates unknown)

Pronounced Petr Zeznoyma. He was educated in England and became professor of theology in Prague from 1397. Initially he was a supporter of Hus, but later turned against him and became an implacable opponent.

ze Znojma, Stanislav [Stanislas of Znojmo or of Znaim] (c. 1351–1414)

Pronounced Stanislaf Zeznoyma. A theologian at the University of Prague. He taught Hus, Jerome and Štěpán z Pálče. Initially he was an enthusiastic teacher of Wycliffe's doctrines and supported Hus. In 1408 Stanislav and Štěpán z Pálče attended the Council of Pisa, but both were captured and imprisoned for some time. After this, he began gradually to deviate from Wycliffe's teachings and ended up attacking them and Hus. King Václav IV banished him from Bohemia when he refused to attend meetings aimed at restoring peace to Bohemia.

Zwingli, Huldrych or Ulrich (1484–1531)

Swiss Reformer.

Erratum
Page 202, line 3:
The date 1518 should be 1521